# God
## Never Wastes
## a
# Hurt

*A widow's journey
through Grief, Faith,
& Hope*

# Susan Daniel

WESTBOW
PRESS®
A DIVISION OF THOMAS NELSON
& ZONDERVAN

Scripture quotations marked (NIV) are taken from the Holy Bible, New
International Version®, NIV®. Copyright © 1973, 1978, 1984, 2011 by Biblica,
Inc.™ Used by permission of Zondervan. All rights reserved worldwide.
www.zondervan.com The "NIV" and "New International Version" are trademarks
registered in the United States Patent and Trademark Office by Biblica, Inc.™

WestBow Press books may be ordered through booksellers or by contacting:

WestBow Press
A Division of Thomas Nelson & Zondervan
1663 Liberty Drive
Bloomington, IN 47403
www.westbowpress.com
1 (866) 928-1240

Because of the dynamic nature of the Internet, any web addresses or
links contained in this book may have changed since publication and
may no longer be valid. The views expressed in this work are solely those
of the author and do not necessarily reflect the views of the publisher,
and the publisher hereby disclaims any responsibility for them.

Any people depicted in stock imagery provided by Thinkstock are models,
and such images are being used for illustrative purposes only.
Certain stock imagery © Thinkstock.

ISBN: 978-1-9736-1399-2 (sc)

Library of Congress Control Number: 2018900288

Print information available on the last page.

WestBow Press rev. date: 01/26/2018

# Acknowledgements

God gets all the glory for this book. These are all His words. He used me to write these words about how He used Ron, an ordinary man, to do His work. Ron and I were just living our lives, not having a clue that God was orchestrating this story for me to tell you now. It's all God. It's not me at all. He just used me.

Mom and Dad, you are both amazing. When I married your baby boy, we had no clue we would be without him four years later. My parents are in Heaven. God knew I still needed parents, so He gave me the best on the planet. You have both been such a blessing to me, and very supportive of this book. Some things in here are very personal and tough. You'll never know how much you both mean to me. Thank you so much for including me in your family. I love you both to the moon and back a zillion times!

Frank Eschmann, Life Care Pastor at FBC (Fellowship Bible Church), little did you know that when you taught that last session on Recycling Pain--The Sharing Choice, on July 9, 2013, that this book would come out of that lesson, when you asked "How can we use our pain to help others?" And that others in the group would suggest writing this book. They don't know the impact that had on me. I remember you said, "God never wastes a hurt." That stuck in my head and is now the first part of the title of this book. Who knew this would all happen? God knew.

FBC pastors, staff, volunteers, and my church family, thank you for all your love, support, and friendship. You all have been amazing and have helped me so much in this grief process. It's so nice to know

I'm not alone. Thanks for teaching me about what a relationship with Jesus is like. Thanks for making me think, laugh, and cry. There are too many of you to mention. To avoid risking leaving anyone out, I am saying "Thank You" to each and every one of you. Serving and attending at FBC is like a family reunion every week! It truly helps keep me going through this crazy life. There is no way to thank you all. Just know that each one of you has been a blessing to me.

To my friends and family, many of you don't even know about this book, but you have helped support me in many ways. Each of you has a special place in my heart and God has put you there for a reason. Thank you all for putting up with my craziness, my tantrums, my wild dreams, and for being a part of this journey. I love you all more than I can say. We may not always stay in contact or see each other very often. Some of you may wish we didn't! Just know that you are in my thoughts and heart and that I love you all very much.

To my professional helpers, I'm not naming names and am not ashamed to say I get therapy every week, most of the time, twice a week--one for regular stuff, one for grief counseling. You two have given me tremendous support in writing this book and with life stuff. The widows group has really helped me with this new normal stuff, and to know that I am not alone. Thank you both for all your time and listening to me talk!

Charity Delay, you are like a daughter to me. I had no clue what you would create when I asked you to do this cover. All I told you was tears down the left side, blue sky, white puffy clouds, rainbow, and the title. In no time flat, you sent me a picture and it made me cry in a public place! It's beautiful and I love the little butterfly you added. You truly have a gift from God. I am very thankful He put you in my life, for many reasons, but especially to have your creation as the cover for this book. I love you dearly, don't you ever forget it!

Janene Daniel, my awesome sister-in-law! Thank you for your hard work typing part of this book. It means a lot to me to have you included in this process. Thank you for all the times you made me laugh. I love you bunches!

Diane Zimmerman, my friend and sister in Christ, thank you for all the hours of typing, editing, and redoing things in order for this to be published. You saved me big time by knowing how to do all this stuff! You'll never know how much this means to me.

Wyatt Johnston, if only you knew when you were playing with your camera and took Ron's picture that day, how special that picture would become to our family. It is such a blessing to look at it every day and see his grin that we all love and miss so very much. Thank you for allowing others to see it, too.

Thank you for working your technical magic to fix the pictures to be used in this book. You have an amazing gift. I cannot thank you enough!

Elaine Woodard, thank you for coming to my rescue with Author Bio and About The Book. God gave me the words for the book for not for these!

You are an amazing friend and I am so thankful for your help and friendship. You are awesome!

Mahalia Hilts, you have to be the smartest person on the planet!

This book was sitting at Westbow for two years because I did not know anyone at that time to help me. With just a few clicks you placed the pictures where they needed to be.

Then came the corrections. Again, with just a few clicks and it was done!

Thank you for using your technical magic to get this book on its way to being published.

I am so thankful you are my friend!

Patsy Salmon, thank you for taking my Author Picture on the back cover of this book. You know how much I hate having my picture taken!

I really appreciate your patience waiting for mother nature to give us that beautiful day, and your expertise with your camera and for finding just the right spot to capture the look I wanted!

You are awesome and I am blessed to call you my friend.

Debi Sporleder, I cannot tell you how much you mean to me! There are no words to describe how thankful I am that God put you in my life. You are always there for me, and I am grateful.

I am so thankful for your help with the final logistics of making this book finally happen! Thank you for using your technical magic!

I am so very blessed for all of you. Each one of you used your gifts one by one along this journey of making this book become real. Each one of you are amazing and I cannot thank you enough.

God put each one of you in my life for a reason. Thank you for your technical help, your support, encouragement and especially your prayers.

Thank each one of you for helping this story be told, how God Never Wastes a Hurt, so that it may somehow, someway help another person on their grief journey.

I am forever humbled.

# July 9, 2013

Well, tonight was awesome. It is the last night of Finding Hope, Life's Healing Choices, Freedom from Your Hurts, Hang-Ups, and Habits. Tonight was about Choice #8 – The Sharing Choice. Recycling Pain – about how God uses pain in our lives to get our attention, to teach us to depend on Him, and the one that really hit me like a brick – God allows us pain to give us a ministry to others.

"Who comforts us in all our affliction, so that we may be able to comfort those who are in any affliction, with which we ourselves are comforted by God." 2 Corinthians 1:4

> God uses pain to correct us.
> God uses pain to direct us.
> God uses pain to perfect us.
>
> God never wastes a hurt.
>
> We learn to depend on God's love.
> We learn to follow God's word.
> We learn that we really need other people.

Recycling Pain: In order to help others, I must be honest about these five things:

- My feelings.

- My faults.
- My failures.
- My frustrations.
- My fears.

What do I Share?

- I share how pain got my attention.
- I share how I learned from pain.
- I share how God can bring good out of bad.

Romans 8:28 – "And we know that for those who love God all things work together for good for those who are called according to His purpose."

I admit I did not do my homework for tonight. I don't know why, it's not like I didn't have the time. I just didn't. So now I'm going to read it. Right now.

All the other 7 choices are good, important, and necessary. Why did this one smack me in the face? Maybe it's because I had been thinking about how to share my story...my pain. Giving my testimony in front of Tuesday morning Bible Study would be terrifying. I don't like talking in front of others. I LOVE to talk, just not formally in front of a crowd. I would stumble on my words. I would forget what to say. I could write myself notes. I know myself...I would get lost or want to go too fast or think others won't want to hear it. My biggest fear? I would cry. I would cry after the first word or two. So I can't – at least not yet.

One night a few months ago, I couldn't sleep. I was praying, thanking God for everything that day, and well, just everything. I always think Him for using Ron to lead me back to Him. I don't remember everything else. I talk to God all the time about stuff. Big stuff, little stuff, all kinds of stuff. Later, it popped in my head, I needed to write a book. To share my story. I got all excited and as usual, right on cue, Satan got wind of it and started in telling me "You don't know how to do that!" "You can't do that!" "Your story isn't special." "No one would want to read that." "No one would spend money on that." And on and on. So, as usual I gave up that thought, not really realizing it was Satan. I was always told all my life by people "you can't do that!" Every once in a while that thought would pop back in my head. Sometimes it would pop back out as fast, sometimes it would linger and roll around in my brain, sometimes I would think about it and get excited. Sometimes I would tell myself to get together with my author friend and see what she thinks. I thought about it but never did it.

So, back to group tonight. In our groups, one question was "What does the Great Commission mean to you?"

The next question: "How can you do your part?" BINGO!!!

I told my group I didn't know. I told my story – yes, I started to cry, there were only four others there tonight. One asked if I ever blogged or thought about writing a book? BINGO again!!! Bells and whistles and everything! Someone else had that idea!!! Some others agreed, one said "even if it helped one person it would be worth it." The girl who suggested it stated she would read my story. I about cried…again.

So here I am, Choice #8 Recycling Pain and I found hope at Finding Hope. It says "God wants you to yield to Him and allow Him to recycle the pain in your life for the benefit of others."

"The very thing you want least to talk about, the very thing you want to hide in the closet, is the very thing God wants you to share. One of the great things about God is that He never wastes a hurt. And He doesn't want to waste yours."

The big question in this chapter is "Why does God allow pain?"

- God has given us free will.
- God uses pain to get our attention.
- God uses pain to teach us to depend on Him.
- God allows pain to give us a ministry to others. It prepares you to serve.

BOOM!!!

God wants to use and recycle the pain in your life to help others, but you've got to be open and honest about it. If you keep that hurt to yourself, you're wasting it. God wants to recycle your hurts, your hang-ups and your habits to help others.

God is bigger than anyone who hurts you. No matter what other people have done to you, God can recycle it and use it for good. God never wastes a hurt. But you can waste it, if you don't learn from it and share it. Others will be blessed and encouraged if you share the problems and struggles you've gone through. God can and will use your pain to help others, if you let Him.

How can we use our pain to help others?

The simple answer to the question "How can I use my pain to help others?" is to share your story. That's it. It's that simple and that difficult – you share your experiences, your journey, your weaknesses, and how God has gotten you where you are today. As you share, you'll discover a blessing for yourself, in addition to the one you pass on to others. When you share your story, it not only gives hope to others, it brings healing to you. Every time you share your story, you grow a little bit stronger, you experience another measure of healing.

# ACCEPT YOUR MISSION

God has a mission for you. It's called the "Great Commission." The moment you step across the line and become a believer, you become a missionary. You become a part of God's great plan of reaching out to hurting, lost people.

Do you realize there are only two things you can't do in Heaven? One is sin, the other is share the Good News with people who have never heard it. Which of those do you think is the reason God is leaving you on Earth? Obvious, isn't it? BOOM!!!

If you are a believer, it is your responsibility to share in the problems and troubles of other people. This is where our beatitude for this chapter comes in: "Happy are those who are persecuted because they do what God Requires." There is no greater accomplishment in life than helping somebody find the assurance of heaven.

There are people who need to hear your story. God wants to use you. Share your story. Tell your story –

- Be humble – it's basically one beggar telling another beggar where to find bread.
- Be real – be honest about your hurts and faults. Transparent, vulnerable and real. You, too, can help other people by being honest about your hurts. When you are honest about your hurts, the honesty spreads and helps those who hear your story to open up, too.

- <u>Don't lecture</u> – Don't try to argue or force people into Heaven. Just share your story. God wants you to be a witness, not a defense attorney. You may be the only Bible some people will ever read. Some people wouldn't be caught within a hundred yards of a church, so they would probably never hear a sermon. But you have a story they can identify with. You can reach people a pastor never could. Just share what God has done for you, and they will want what you have!

## CONSIDER YOUR BENEFICIARIES

Who could best benefit from hearing your story? The answer is people who are currently experiencing what you have already gone through, people who need to know Christ and the freedom found in Him and who need to know the eight choices found in this book. They might be your peers, your neighbors, or your family. Tell God you're available, then get ready. If you are prepared to share the Good News of how God has worked in your life, God will wear you out!

Can you imagine getting to Heaven and someone saying to you "I'm in Heaven because of you, and I just want to thank you?" Do you think that sharing your story will have been worth it? It will far outlast anything you do in your career, anything you do in your hobby. We're talking <u>Eternal</u> implications – getting people from darkness into light, from hell into Heaven, from an eternity without God, to an eternity with God. People will be thanking you the rest of eternity. There is nothing more significant in life. I believe "God uses ordinary people to do extraordinary things." A quote by my pastors. I believed God used my husband to lead me back to Him and into a relationship with God. I also believe God is using me to tell the story.

# So...I will tell the story...

I was born in Colby, Kansas and lived there till I was 16. My mom taught Sunday school at United Methodist Church all 16 years of my life. I remember having to wear those awful frilly dresses, black patent leather shoes, and ruffled anklets. I had to have my hair curled with those pink spongy curlers Saturday night. I hated that. Hated the dresses, the curlers. Going to church was not fun for me. It was like a fashion show. As long as I can remember, it was about "my dress is prettier than your dress" or "your dress is ugly" or stuff that had nothing to do with God. I went to Vacation Bible School. It was more relaxed, but I always felt like I didn't belong. I was shy. I didn't fit in. I don't remember learning much about God. I know I was baptized as a baby. I did the confirmation thing. I still have the Bible I was given. I remember after Sunday school going to my mom's Sunday school class, then we went to church. I remember the hymnals. I never sang. I lip-synced. I couldn't sing for nothing. Still can't and people don't want me to show them!!! I remember the pastor standing at his podium talking and reading from the Bible. It didn't make sense to me. It wasn't real to me. He didn't just talk about his life or real life. The Bible was complicated to me.

The cool thing was my mom almost always made fried chicken, mashed potatoes and gravy and corn, or pot roast, potatoes and carrots after church. It's really sad that what my mom cooked after church are my good memories of Sundays, except for football. I remember the Broncos when it was about Orange Crush! I remember my grandpa always telling me I didn't have to go to a building to believe in God. After we moved from Colby to Wamego, KS the summer of '75, I attended a few churches through the years but never felt I belonged there. Never felt welcome, didn't fit in, didn't understand. My mother never found a church she liked either. She always played the hymns on her piano and sang along. Those songs annoyed me a lot of the times. Especially the Christmas songs. I hated hearing those songs on the piano, and her and whatever grandkids were around to sing along. And the records...Christmas music from after Thanksgiving to New Year's. Every year, year after year. Now when our worship team plays those hymns and Christmas songs, I cry. I'd give anything to have her here to play her piano and sing again. I miss her so much.

Little did I know when I asked Ron to be my friend on MySpace that God was up to something BIG. Ron and I chatted on MySpace. I remember one of the first things he asked about me was if I believed in God. Of course I believed in God. I just didn't know a lot about God. I always talked to God. I would pray, I believed God loved me and looked after me. I believed a lot of things about God. I had no clue God was going to use Ron or me. I thanked God over and over for Ron. All those years I searched and he lived right down the interstate in Topeka, Kansas. I lived in Manhattan, Kansas. Ron and I met in March, 2007. The night we first met at Carlos O'Kelly's, I knew I found someone different. We were nervous, but we had fun. That July we got married. 7-7-07, that was supposed to be lucky, right? We didn't even think of it that way. That date was picked in honor of my father who was in heaven on his birthday. So my brother gave me away. We got married in Ron's mom and dad's backyard.

I was so happy. I thought God finally was giving me a break from all the years of pain and hardship and that I was going to finally be happy and not alone anymore. Till death do us part, right? I was living in Manhattan, Kansas when we met. Ron grew up in Topeka, Kansas. Being the man he was, he knew I loved my job and wanted to be close to my family. So he moved to Manhattan. Before we were married, he asked me to come to church with him, and meet his parents. Again, God was up to something BIG. Fellowship Bible Church (FBC) was in a metal building on the west side of Topeka. I was very nervous since I had so many times of not fitting in when I went to church other times. Flashbacks of those horrible uncomfortable dresses, shoes, socks and curled hair made me really nervous. Ron assured me I didn't have to dress up for this church. I still did, though. I remember walking in and being greeted by so many people! I remember there were donuts and lemonade! In church? Really? I kept telling Ron, "The Methodists would never do this!"

And people wore jeans, shorts, flip flops? In church? I was definitely impressed. FBC was very small and I stuck out as the newbie, but people were so friendly! In church?!?! And there was a band? Drums, keyboard and guitars – loud! In church?? Oh, the Methodists would NEVER hear of this! What happened to the choirs with people singing in their quivering voices that I couldn't understand? Wow – awesome music _and_ friendly people, _and_ donuts, _and_ lemonade, _and_ dressed down? Then the message. I don't remember everything that was said, but I do remember that Pastor Joe _talked_ about real life stuff. He even made sense, he made it interesting, he made me enjoy church. He made it an awesome experience. I remember he said he wasn't perfect. Wow! My pastor never would have stood up in church and admitted he wasn't perfect. No way! Joe also said "God doesn't care what you wear as long as you come." Really? A pastor said that? I wanted more. I was hooked that very first service. Oh yeah, Ron's parents? THE most awesome parents God ever made!!!

When we lived in Manhattan, we came to FBC when we could. Ron wanted to go to church every Sunday, so he searched online for churches in Manhattan. We tried three or four. I remember him spending so much time reading about the doctrine and if they talked about salvation. Salvation? Doctrine? I thought we just needed to know the times of service and the address. Then he started talking about tithing in the budget. Tithing? I remember putting money in the dish at church in Colby, but I didn't understand what it was all about. I didn't know it was about being God's money and how, if we tithe, God blesses us and will always meet our needs. Hmmm...

We started going to a small church, Crestview Christian Church. They were very friendly, Pastor Devin also wore jeans and shirts not even tucked in, and he talked about real life stuff and about God and guess what? Devin isn't perfect either!!!

This God thing was really getting interesting! I even joined a prayer warrior group. My first church group since youth group! I remembered Devin talking about how he wanted people who went there to be baptized, and they had to be baptized to join the church. Well, I didn't understand cause I was baptized as a baby. Why did I need to be baptized again? Well, after Ron explained it to me, I decided to be baptized. I am terrified of water, and he was going to put my head under water? I had to stand in like a tank full of water? I was so afraid! I'm so glad I did it though!!

At FBC, Ron was involved in the tech team. He loved learning how to run sound and lights and all that techie stuff I don't understand. He really missed FBC. He volunteered to serve on tech team at Crestview. But, his heart and passion was in Topeka at FBC.

In May, 2008, less than a year of being married, I lost my job. I had worked there 12 years and dearly loved my co-workers and especially my clients. It was being closed down. I couldn't find another job. Ron wanted to move to Topeka. I hated Topeka. Too big, too much crime, way too much crime. I didn't think we would be safe there. There wasn't K-State Football!!! I loved Manhattan, my family was all in that area round Manhattan. I was not a happy camper. I did love FBC and missed it, too. But, still....leaving Manhappiness for Topeka? I went, but went kicking and screaming!

Before Ron moved to Manhattan, he attended a small group at FBC. Naturally, I had no clue what that was. Ron wanted to start going back there and they all welcomed me with open arms. I felt stupid. I felt inadequate reading from the Bible and talking about the lesson. Oh, yeah, to back up, Ron gave me a Bible with a zippered cover for our first Christmas, December 2007, burgundy, his favorite color. I reminded him to write in it that it was from him, and the date. I'm glad I did. I still look at his writing. I still cry.

So I had my own Bible and attended Bible studies. Ron was happy to be back at FBC with the Tech Team. By this time, FBC had moved into their new building at 10th and Urish. It's beautiful. Ron had helped work on it some before we met. I knew this place was special. It felt right. I loved the messages. I understood them. They were delivered in a way that makes them real, that I can relate to. I learned the gospel. It's more than gospel music! I learned about salvation. I learned I can never be good enough, try hard enough, be perfect. I can't buy my way into heaven. It's not about how hard I work or how nice I am or how much money I give the church. Wow! What a relief cause that's what I was taught in Colby. It was about my works, trying to be good enough and so on. This gospel and salvation thing was pretty cool! Sure wish I would have learned that years ago! My life would have been a lot different. But, like I said, God had a plan and was up to something big.

I enjoyed Bible studies and small group. I still felt stupid and lost, but I was learning and listening and paying attention. We took a Perspectives Class together. Man, was that deep! It opened my eyes to things I never thought about before. There was a lot of reading and homework and Ron and I spent HOURS soaking it all up. The speakers were awesome. Ron and I talked about how we thought God was going to use us because neither one of us felt led to go to another country.

Our church started doing an L-3 Journal where we read scriptures every day and journal our thoughts. Ron was very faithful reading the Word every day. He would get up early to make sure he gave God his first and his best. Me? I did it, but I am sad to say I did not get up extra early. I am doing much better at it now.

At one point, I can't even remember when now, things got bad. Ron was waiting to get approved for disability. Bills kept coming, I always had doctor appointments and it got too much for Ron. He got mad at God. He turned his back on God. He quit tech team. Ron was always the first one to volunteer when they needed someone. He didn't want to go to church. He quit reading his bible and stopped doing his L-3. Life was not pretty during this time. All this time till now, he was the spiritual leader in our house. He was helping and encouraging me. Now, he wouldn't go to small group either. He was miserable, but too stubborn to admit it. I don't remember how long this lasted. It seemed like forever. Things seemed to be falling apart. If I remember right, our small group leader called Ron and asked him to lunch. He is an amazing man, a very godly man. I don't know what was said, but Ron came home a much happier person. They even made a phone call to the Tech Arts Director and got him back on the team.

Ron loved serving in The Mountain, the children's program. Ron loved doing the sound, lights and video. He wanted to learn as much as possible. His dream was to be a part of the tech team in the Worship Center. But, he felt the Mountain was his baby. He finally found a place where he felt accepted, despite his mild cerebral palsy, which limited some things he could do. Kids and people made fun of him all his life. Now he could serve God through his love of music and learning tech stuff. He would spend hours on the computer studying assignments for the tech team. He loved to help set up and tear down in the Worship Center and special events. He felt at home serving God and being available to Him.

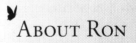

# ABOUT RON

Ron was unlike anyone I had met before. When we would talk on MySpace, I loved how respectful he was. How polite. When he said he would call at a certain time, he called, on the dot! Not a minute late. When he said he would be at my place, he was there on the dot, if not early. This was going to drive me crazy down the road! He always had to be someplace 15 minutes early or right on time. Well…me…fifteen minutes before we had to be there, I would start to get ready! Poor man, he was so patient but I know this drove him crazy! When we went places, he opened the doors – always. When in line, I had to go in front of him. When getting in the car – he opened the door. Wow! This was weird and very cool. It was hard to get used to. Guess I felt like I didn't deserve it. When getting gas – he always pumped gas. That was very weird to me cause I had been a single parent forever and always had to do it myself. I got used to this fast! And got spoiled rotten. Ron loved to cook and clean. He was meticulous. I hated, and still hate, to cook and clean. I almost felt guilty when he cooked or cleaned cause I was used to doing it. Poor guy, he was so organized. Me? Not even close! I'm a "pile" person. I never understood how people do not have piles! I would ask him where he puts things if he didn't have piles. Being the practical person he was, he said something like "where it belongs!" Hmmm…what a concept! I've heard of people like that, but never lived with one! I know my piles had to secretly bug him. He never got mad at me for my piles, and I had piles! But they were organized chaos piles. He could not understand piles. He was so practical and I'm the dreamer. This would be a problem, and hilarious at the same time. He was a planner, I'm a spontaneous free spirit. The really hard part was when he started talking about a budget!! A budget? What? I've heard of those, but being the spontaneous free spirit, they totally mess with whatever idea pops in my head at that moment. Boy, did he have his work cut out for him! He had been through Dave Ramsey's Financial Peace Program before we met. There was one being offered at FBC, and he thought we needed to take it together. Boy, was that an experience! That's where I found out there was a name for our differences in thinking. He was a nerd and me – the free spirit. That's why he acted like that! Talking about budgeting, saving, all that stuff! He made the budget. He spent HOURS getting down to zero based. He would ask me what I thought about this or that. Well, of course I didn't have a clue, so I agreed most of the time. The hard part was sticking to it. We most always went grocery shopping and to Wal-Mart together – once a week. What? I had to think ahead that far? Wow! That was hard!

He taught me that generic brands were really okay! I grew up with my mom having to have everything name brand. Everything!! Boy, that was hard changing to generic, but you know what? Things really didn't taste that bad!?! What a concept, buying something cheaper!!! I remember the first month or so leaving the store in tears cause we went over a few bucks. One time was only a dollar or so and I felt horrible! I was happy when he budgeted in date night eating out once a month. Money was tight, so once a month was better than nothing.

And then there were the dogs. When he married me, he inherited two grown kids, two grandkids, and two dogs. Jake was 110-pound Black Lab I rescued from the shelter in Manhattan when he was a year and a half. Dakota was a Golden Retriever I got when he was 3 months old. They were big dogs, so they ate a lot. And had to have shots, and when we moved to Topeka, there was something in the back yard that Jake was allergic to. So, he had to have medicine every Spring till hard freeze. Antihistamine and antibiotics. Ron somehow found a way to budget food and meds for them. He was <u>NOT</u> a dog person. He was one of those cat people. Again, I did not understand his way of thinking. Cats could care less what we want. They only think of themselves, what they want and when they want it. When we met, he had a cat, Cassie. She was old and a Calico. She hated me. I was the intruder. When she was moved to Manhattan, she really hated me! She was used to it being her and Ron, that's it. No one else. Now she was moved, and had to deal with me and Jake and Dakota. Jake loved cats. He loved them so much he was like a bull in a china shop trying to get the cat! So, they had to be separated. Cassie soon had to be put to sleep due to kidney failure. Ron cried like a baby.

When we moved to Topeka, some friends in our small group had a cat they needed a home for. Ron wanted it, so we got him. His name was Morris and he was beautiful. He lived up to his name alright. He hated me, hated the dogs. He had been an indoor-only cat, but decided he wanted to be an indoor/outdoor cat. Well, I sure didn't appreciate his gifts of dead squirrels he would leave at the back door!! I get grossed out easily and dead squirrels were gross to me, certainly NOT a special present like Morris seemed to think! My dogs chased them, but never killed them!

I don't remember how long we had Morris. I do remember when he wanted out and never came back. Our neighbors had cats and said they had lost some, too. They discovered a possum family in their neighbor's yard. Again, Ron lost a cat and was devastated. He really tried to love Jake and Dakota. I know they frustrated him. They weren't independent like the cats. They had to be let outside, they ate a lot, drank a lot and shed a lot! And Jake, well, bless his heart, he didn't understand he was a big dog and Ron was a thin man. Jake thought he was a lap dog. He would crawl up on Ron's lap and stretch out and get all comfy! Ron played with him and humored Jake, but I really do not think he appreciated the 110-pound dog on his lap! Jake also had a barking problem. I say he heard dogs or noises in other states cause he would bark, and bark, and bark at things we never heard! Ron tolerated Jake and Dakota even though he had to share the bathroom with Jake's food bowl and the big water bowl. Our bathroom wasn't huge, but Jake was. And they drank a lot…and left trails of dripping water when they were done. It was annoying, but they were my babies and he knew they were part of the package deal. Poor guy.

And, also the practical part of him drove me crazy cause I am the dog lover and I discovered the pet category on Craigslist. I was a Craigslist Junkie! Hi, my name is Susan and I'm a Craigslist Junkie! I love dogs and especially Labs. I love their temperament, gentle spirit, and, of course, their eyes! But, then again, I could look in almost every dog's eyes and want to bring them home. I would find a dog and happily show him the adorable pic and read how awesome it was. Being the practical person he was, he would burst my bubble instantly by saying something practical like "We can't afford another dog" or "We don't need another dog" or "We don't have room for another dog." What? What was the problem? The dog needed a home – we had a home – no problem! We had a small home, and, yes, Jake and Dakota were big dogs and when they would stretch out on the floor you had to step over them--don't want to disturb them if they were resting! I would tell him "there's room for it over there, or there. We still have floor space!" He didn't understand! I just didn't see the problem.

Then, when my mother unexpectedly passed away, I was a basket case. Full-blown basket case. I was the baby. My father had passed in 1998. I was Daddy's girl and I still miss him deeply. This was 2009. I cried and cried and cried. She passed in September of '09. My grief was so bad, for so long. Ron knew I wanted a Chocolate Lab. He thought maybe that would help me heal. So, it didn't take me long to start looking. I found them all over the country. I didn't see the problem going to Oklahoma or Colorado or wherever there was a Chocolate Lab. If it needed a home, we needed to get it! That was my way of thinking. Being the practical person he was, he gently stated it had to be close to here. Fine. What was going to happen to those other dogs far away if we didn't rescue them? Who would save them from the kill shelters? I truly wished we had a lot of land to save those poor Labs! Ron was very thankful we didn't have land. He and others said "other people" will adopt them. I still don't know how they knew that. I wasn't convinced, but hey, I would find one closer. I found a pic of a terrified puppy in a kill shelter an hour from here. It didn't look like a Chocolate Lab, totally, but it was scared and needed rescued! So, we drove there and saw her. She was in a pen with a Chocolate Lab puppy, bouncing all over the place. The lady had to pick this puppy up and bring her out of her pen to meet us. The other one was so playful, pulling my hair and was so cute. Ron said it was too busy. This other pup was shaking and was afraid of us. I picked her up, looked in her eyes and convinced myself we were going to save her. Ron did the usual grinning, slowly shaking his head, and rolling his eyes like I was crazy or something. Well, I told him ever since we met I was! That poor dog never moved in my arms all the way home. Of course, I held her. She shook like she was so scared. I was determined to rescue and love this dog!

Remember, Ron was not the dog person. He tolerated them, but still loved cats. I never got him over that!

We named this dog Luv. It took her a long time to warm up to us. She was fine with Jake and Dakota. We soon discovered she was NOT a Lab. Not even close. She was always on guard, always pacing. Never the laid- back lab. The more I learned about her, the more I was mad at the kill shelter for not knowing she was a Vizsla. Not a Lab. Not a drop. And she did not like Ron. She growled and barked at him all the time. She must have had a male hurt her before, or something. She wanted nothing to do with him. Ron said she had to go. I looked all over for rescues. I refused to put her on Craigslist or take her to a kill shelter. I tried and tried, and all the rescues around were full or could not take her for some reason. Then, we were blessed that Ron's brother and wife in Indianapolis were visiting. She is a huge animal person and fell in love with Luv. We convinced Ron's brother that Luv needed to go home with them. Let's just say Luv is perfectly happy and totally spoiled rotten in Indianapolis! I am happy because I know where she is and see pics of her and have been there twice to see her. She still barks at me.

I cried and felt like such a doggy mommy failure, but God was good and found her the best home ever! Ron said we were done with dogs...yeah, right! I will never be done with dogs and am still praying for that cabin with land so I can rescue Labs!

One of the coolest things Ron started doing after we were married was read to me at bedtime. Not just a bedtime story, but somehow he knew I needed to learn more about God and this was a way God used him again. He read the Left Behind series. Every night, a chapter; or if I didn't like the way that chapter ended by leaving me hanging, I would beg him to read another one. Of course, that chapter would end the same way, but Ron was a very routine, practical person and seemed to think that cause the alarm would go off in the morning that he couldn't read all night. Practical people really annoy me sometimes.

Man, did I ever learn a lot! Rapture? Never heard of it. God's seal? Never heard of it. And on and on of "never heard of it," or "Oh, that's what that means!" Those light bulb moments. If only he knew, REALLY knew, God was using him to teach me. And if only he knew how important those times were to me when I would hang on every word, or cry or get mad at whatever was happening in that chapter. If only he knew how I treasure those times. Bedtime isn't the same, and never will be.

After reading the whole series to me, one chapter (maybe two if I threw a big enough fit) at a time, we needed something else to read. Before finishing the series, my mom went to Heaven. Like I said before, I was a basket case. So when we needed another book to read, I asked him to read Heaven by Randy Alcorn. I had asked him to get that book for me for Christmas after mom passed. So he started reading it. It wasn't filled with the drama of Left Behind, but I learned a lot.

Again, God was using him. The last page he read to me was almost exactly half way through.

After he passed, I would go to the cemetery and read out loud to him about Heaven. That was weird. That Christmas after he passed, I bought Heaven for my family and for the pastors – all of them – at FBC. I included a card asking them to please finish reading this with me. I also put in a scroll about Christmas in heaven. Yeah, that was a rough Christmas. But, it helped start the healing process. Ron never let me read. He always had to read, even if he was really tired. So, it was kind of cool going to his grave, plopping down on the ground and telling him now I was going to read!

# July 17, 2013

Today I met with my friend who just happens to be an author! See, God was up to something again--seems like He always is; I'm just not always paying attention!

See, last Spring at Finding Hope, on Tuesday nights, I went there hoping and expecting to be in the group for families of people who suffer from PTSD, like my son does. I wanted to meet other moms who deal with this. No one showed up for this group. NO ONE!! I was like "Great, what group do I do now?" I already did Griefshare after Ron passed away. Then I did Boundaries. The pastor suggested I sit in on the Anger group. I felt pretty lost and like I didn't fit in there, but I obeyed, and went. I do not feel I have an anger problem. But, I went, and I learned a lot. But what God was up to, I think, was that the leader of this group wrote the study guide and book and was using it in the group. She understands PTSD. She donates a percentage of her book money to veterans. I thought that was awesome! She understood PTSD and understood me. Anyway, when a person in group last week suggested I write a book, I thought "I know an author!"

So, we met today and I explained how powerful the last night of Finding Hope was. She had missed that night. I told her about it and let her read what all I had written so far. She did exactly what I prayed for! She laughed at times and almost teared up at times. She reaffirmed that this needs to be written. My story is worth telling. She even stayed longer than she planned on cause she was not going to stop reading. So laugh, smile, tear up, and hold her attention. Yep, that's what I prayed for.

After getting home and taking my dogs out, I heard sirens. There are always sirens. They make me hold my breath a minute. They came closer and closer. I never heard them in my complex before. I saw they were two doors down from me. There are four townhomes in my building. I know my neighbor beside me and on the end. This person was only two doors from me and I don't know her. That needs to change!

I saw the ambulance, then the fire truck. My heart sank. I saw them get out the gurney and leave it outside while EMS went inside. I stared at those lights, then the gurney. I was overwhelmed. I knew I was gonna have to write about those horrible, yet God-filled, four days. The major piece to my journey. The day my world fell apart, and another day God showed up – BIG TIME.

I knew I was gonna have to write about it. It just never felt like the right time. Not until I heard those sirens, saw the lights, saw the ambulance and fire truck two doors down from me. And when I saw the gurney. So, here I go. This is gonna be hard. I'm gonna cry, maybe you will cry with me…maybe you have experienced something like this, too. I'm horrible with times and dates. I don't remember yesterday very well.

Ron was working part-time at a home health agency. He was a Transitional Living Specialist. He had applied for and was granted disability. He was on a program so he could still work. See, even though Ron had mild cerebral palsy, that didn't slow him down…ever. He was sick a lot as a child. His parents were told when he was born that he had a hole in his heart.

That he had Epstein's Anomaly. That he wouldn't live to be a teenager.

Ron showed them! Ron was the kind of person who did not like to be told that he could not do something because of his disability. He would try and try himself and maybe he had to do it a different way, but would not give up until HE decided he could not do something. As a child, (Ron and his parents told me stories of his Evil Knievel stunts) he was always getting hurt before a vacation, always pushing the limits just to prove to himself and others that he could do something. Because of the hole in his heart, Ron had to go to Children's Mercy and doctor appointments for cerebral palsy. Ron had a horrible fear of needles. He had told me this before, but I didn't really know his fear of needles till this happened. When he was 21, he was told the hole in his heart had healed and he no longer needed check-ups. Since Ron was otherwise healthy and because of his fear of needles, he wouldn't go to the doctor unless it was to the ER for some accident that required attention. I was the opposite. In 2004 I was diagnosed with fibromyalgia. I practically lived at the doctor's offices or ER for pain I couldn't stand, or migraines--bad migraines. I was used to needles, no big deal.

In 2011, the nagging wife in me wanted him to get a physical. He fought it, being the practical person--if he wasn't sick, why should he get a physical? Well, cause I said so! I just wanted to know if everything was OK. He was 45. The men on his mom's side died in their 40's from heart problems. There was also Factor Five. We didn't understand it, but I wanted to know if he had it. So, Ron (being Ron) gave into going to the doctor for a physical. I secretly think he did it to prove me wrong, that he was fine, and I would drop it.

Since Ron rarely went to the doctor, he didn't have a primary care doctor. He found one and I went to the appointment with him. He almost always went to my appointments with me. His doc was very nice and seemed to know his stuff. He checked Ron out, listened to his heart, then he listened again. The doctor told Ron he wanted him to see a cardiologist here in town. The cardiologist seemed concerned and ordered an echo of his heart. Oh yeah, his primary care doc took blood! It took me holding his legs and a lab tech holding his arms just to get his blood. He was so afraid of the needle. He would hyperventilate. I kept telling him it was okay. That would be like someone holding me down and putting a spider or snake on me! The day of the echo, it took a lab tech, Ron's mom and dad and me to hold arms and legs for blood. Echo showed good and bad. Good news was he did not have Epstein's Anomaly; that is why he was 45 years old and still alive when he wasn't supposed to live to be a teenager. Bad news was the hole in his heart was not closed up, as he was told years ago. There was a .8 cm hole and moderate-to-severe right atrial enlargement. The cardiologist referred us to KU Med to discuss closing the hole.

Ron's mom and dad drove us to meet with the doc. He was very nice and spent time explaining things to us, answering our questions. The cardiologist gave Ron the option of open-heart surgery or patching the hole. Ron was not about lying around and doing nothing! It was hard to keep him down for anything, so since open-heart meant longer recovery time, that was not an option to him. I didn't really like that idea, but respected his decision.

He had to have blood work done; because of his fear of needles, he requested medication to help calm him and lessen the anxiety. It calmed him all right! Yep! I took pics of him out like a light bulb, waiting for lab. It might have been mean of me, but we had a good laugh at him. I still have those pics. One of them is when we were laughing at him, he stuck his tongue out at me. Aw, yep, here come the tears. Having to go through these papers for dates and info is hard. I haven't looked at these for a long time.

# The Last Week of Ron's Life

On September 26, 2011, we arrived at KU Med for Ron's surgery to patch the hole in his heart. Staff was nice, made it seem like it really wasn't a big deal, they do it all the time. It was a big deal to us. Ron's aunt and uncle, who lived nearby, came up and waited with us. We waited and waited and waited...

Then came the news. Ron had a hole in his heart, but he also had 3 others. One was larger than the one they knew he had. Then another one, and a very tiny one. The doctor stated he thought about opening him up, but knew that was not what Ron wanted. So, the doctor patched 2 holes with one patch, one patch for another hole, and the tiny one was not a problem and did not need patched.

The plan was for me to stay with Ron, and his mom and dad would return the next day to bring us home. Really? You find three holes, patch him up and kick him out the next day? I shouldn't talk bad about Ron, but he was NOT a pleasant patient! When he came out of sedation, he kept trying to sit up, get up, move around. Like I said, he wasn't an easy man to keep down. Nursing staff was very nice, but firm--he had to be still for awhile. He was trying to pull the IV out. IV meant NEEDLE! Ron was very grumpy and annoyed when I was constantly reminding him he had to lie still. He called me "bossy" or "mothering him." It was not a fun time. Then he started having severe back pain. The surgeon was called in and ordered an echo. It all came out okay, but something seemed very wrong--he was in so much pain. I was happy the meds to sedate him helped. I tried to sleep on a cot beside him, but just as I dozed off, he would start to wake up and try and move. When morning came, I was pretty tired from no sleep and him being mad at me for not letting him get up. I knew his recovery time was gonna be hard. But, I had no clue what was gonna happen next.

# September 27, 2011

The ride home was horrible. Ron was NOT happy the doctor told his parents and me about the surgery and not him, or him first. It was hard not to laugh, because we all witnessed the surgeon telling Ron what he found and what he did. Ron didn't remember because he had just come out of a long surgery and was sedated! Duh!!! But nooooo, Ron wasn't having it! Couldn't convince him that the doctor wasn't hiding something from him. It was a rough day at home cause he just wasn't letting it go. He did rest as he was told by doctors. He still called me bossy, worrying too much, trying to mother him and on and on. He rested, but he didn't like it. It was almost like they changed his personality in the surgery room.

Wednesday was much better. He was much nicer, feeling good, wanted to drive, wanted to go to work pulling weeds and doing yard work at our small group leader's home. He didn't do it, but he sure wanted to! He played with Savannah, his kitten that I just remembered I didn't write about yet. And Sophie. More on that later.

Anyway, Wednesday was a good day. He didn't call me bossy or say I was being mean. It was just very hard for him to stay still and follow doctor's orders. But he did. I made sure of that, bossy or not. He did his L-3 Journal, his Bible study, watched TV, just stuff.

Thursday, my world came crashing down. He had an appointment with his primary care doc to get something to help him stop smoking. He got up, did his L-3 journal, read his Bible, ate and took a shower. In that order. His L-3 and Bible came first. He totally believed in giving God his first and his best, not his last and his leftovers. When Ron came out of the shower, he did something he rarely ever did. He admitted he did not feel good. He put his hands to his neck and upper chest and said it felt weird, there was pressure.

Uh oh….He immediately called KU doc, told them how he felt. Nurse told him to have me to take him to the ER NOW!!!

Ron went to sit on the ottoman and could not sit down. He said there was pressure in neck and upper chest, so he was kinda sitting, with legs out, almost lying down. I told him I needed to call 911. He said "call mom and dad first." Those were his last words…ever. He said "call mom and dad first." I did. I called his mom and said I was calling 911. She said his dad was close and would call him. As soon as I hung up, I heard sounds I never want to hear again. He made this gurgling sound, then noises like he was gasping for air. His eyes went back, he was limp. Of course, I was still on the phone with 911 and was yelling for them to hurry up!!! We lived only a few blocks from a fire station. It felt like hours for them to get there.

I forgot the front door was locked. Ron's dad beat EMS there. We had Ron on the floor; he was unresponsive. His dad was calling his name… nothing. Absolutely nothing. I told 911 about Ron having patches on his heart and wouldn't CPR hurt them? I finally heard sirens. Finally, they were there. I can't even remember everything--it happened so fast, yet so slow. I explained the patches, KU Med, all that stuff. They hurried him out of our small living room. I remember seeing our neighbors standing outside watching as they put him in the ambulance, and Ron's dad drove us to the ER. And the ambulance took the long way. Seriously, they went the long way! Why would they do that? When we got to the ER, we told them who we were and Ron was there and KU said to have docs call them.

It seemed like forever before they called Ron's dad and me back into this room to wait for the ER doc to come talk to us. I'd never been in a room like this before. Something wasn't right and wasn't going to be right. I called to talk to our pastor--he was on other line. I told the church secretary what happened. She put the Tech Arts Director on, and he said he'd tell the pastor and he would be right there--and he was there, and fast! Ron's mom got there. The doctor finally came to talk to us. He had been working on Ron. Ron had coded when in the ambulance and when he got to the ER. They were trying to save his life. I don't even remember all that was said except they were doing their best. They moved us to some waiting room. I don't remember which one; we were in so many that day. They said they wanted to put a temporary pacemaker in him, but he kept coding. They did some test and found out he was filling up with blood. Our pastor came, and friends from Ron's mom and dad's small group came. Little did we know that it was the beginning of how full those waiting rooms were going to be.

I remember telling our pastor and others that Ron did his L-3, read his Bible, took a shower. He was fine!! He was fine, and then everything went very, very wrong--very, very fast. When I mentioned that Ron did his L-3 journal, the pastor said, "John 7:37-38, "On the last and greatest day of the feast, Jesus stood and said in a loud voice, "If anyone is thirsty, let him come to me and drink. Whoever believes in me as the scripture has said streams of living water will flow from within him." That's exactly what Ron wrote that morning, his last L-3 journal entry, September 29, 2011. I remember they said we could see him as they rushed him in to put the pacemaker in. As they were rushing him by, the nurse gave me his wedding ring, his chain I gave him, and the chain with the link that was given out at church a few Easters ago that Ron never took off. One of the challenges the staff had was that one of the cardiologist surgeons was on vacation and the other was already in surgery. They called the one on vacation in to work on him until the other one was done with surgery. We couldn't wait. Ron had coded so many times. I remember we had been in three waiting rooms by now. Our little group of supporters was growing, and fast. We were now in the main surgery waiting room. They said they had to open him up, do a bypass, and other stuff I can't remember and don't understand. By now, there were so many people with us--my daughter and son and sister and brother were there. People from our small group, friends from church, and people from Ron's mom and dad's small group were there. I was amazed at how people dropped everything to be there for us. Other pastors showed up from our church, other staff. At one time, I counted 25 people just for us, and praying for Ron. We owned that surgery waiting room! People came, people left, people came back again. People who had small children came to be with us. I was overwhelmed. I was in a daze, I was scared, I was sad, I was devastated. I was a mess! Doctors would come talk to us. I remember one told us many times, "It will take a miracle to save him." We were all praying for a miracle.

Remember I mentioned my small group? God really knew what He was doing. God put us in a small group whose leader is a doctor and his wife had worked as a cardiac ICU nurse. BAM!!!! God gave us these people because we needed them, big time. They were there, explaining what the doctors and nurses told us. I still don't remember. I do remember all of us 20-some people piling into the room for the doctors to talk to us. I think the doctors were amazed at our big group. I still cry and just shake my head when I think about those long hours, waiting. I think that surgery was 5-6 hours long. Many people had been with us since morning. Some stayed with us late into the night.

Ron's patches eroded his aorta. That's what happened. He was bleeding inside from one of the patches cutting his aorta. They worked and worked and worked on him. Staff was so tired. The doctors were tired. We could see they were being so touched by this. They were trying so hard to save his life. Ron was only 45 years old. Ron was NOT a quitter. Ron was a fighter and always proved doctors wrong. I prayed this time he would still fight and still prove them wrong. One huge problem besides the patch eroding the aorta was the amount of time his brain was without oxygen. All the time waiting on EMS, all the times he coded. There wasn't any brain activity. We were told we needed to wait 72 hours to see if there would be any brain activity. After hours of waiting for surgery to be over, after countless awesome prayer warriors visiting us or praying all over the country--Indiana, Vegas, Texas, Colorado, Iowa, Alaska and I'm sure I'm forgetting other places--who put him on churches' prayer chains. It was mind-blowing how so many people from all over were telling their friends and families, so people who didn't even know him were praying. I was praying God would hear all those prayers and not take him from us.

Upstairs in Cardiac ICU, the staff was so awesome! I know we drove them batty because there were so many of us, all wanting to see him. That was so horribly hard. Seeing him hooked up to the vent, tubes, wires, IV, machines--and him. Ron, kept alive by machines. I can still hear the noise of the vent. I remember that noise from when my dad was on the vent before he passed. That's a noise you don't ever wanna hear again, but can't forget. And the needles in him. He couldn't feel it, and we knew if he ever did wake up, he would rip them out instantly! But, he didn't wake up. We prayed, we talked to him, we cried, we prayed some more. He didn't move, nothing but eyes blinking sometimes like he was gonna open them. And he would do it when certain people were talking. We would see them blink and get hopeful, only to be told it was some nerve movement or something, but no brain activity.

That first night in ICU was so hard. We were all so very tired and the chairs didn't make out into beds. So we pulled chairs together. Ron's mom and dad, my sister, my daughter, my son on the floor, Ron's mom and dad's friends, and me. People finally left around 1 or 2 a.m. and we tried to sleep on chairs pulled together. I don't think many of us actually slept. We were hoping the doctor would tell us what we wanted to hear in the morning. That didn't happen. No change, no good news. Our small group leader had a friend who has a prayer team. I can't remember how many people came with that team. They didn't know us or Ron. They just knew Ron needed to be prayed over. We appreciated that so much.

We could tell that most of the staff were Christians. You can just tell. I think it would be horribly hard to work there, with that emotional intensity, and not be a Christian. They supported us and all the prayer warriors. They were so kind and patient. At least most of them. Some weren't so understanding or compassionate. They had a very tough job. Ron wasn't their only patient, but most of the staff said he was their favorite. Hmmm…he was their favorite and he couldn't even speak or acknowledge them. Believe me, he wasn't the staff's favorite patient in KU Med! Maybe it was his age, maybe it was his story, maybe it was because he was a Christian and was surrounded by loving, grieving

Christians. Maybe the staff needed us. Maybe they needed what we had, what we gave them. I could never do their job.

We noticed in our time of owning the Cardiac ICU waiting room that others waiting and visiting friends and loved ones didn't have the support we did. Maybe a few people, maybe no one. So my in-laws and others would go talk to them. I could tell they appreciated it and wanted and needed someone to talk to. I think they wanted what we had. We were worried, scared, grieving, praying, but we had the love of Jesus in us and they saw it. Some people may have been annoyed by so many of us there. Sometimes we were loud, sometimes we cried. I cried. I cried a lot. Ron was my best friend, my soul mate, and I was terrified I was gonna lose him. I couldn't let myself even think that thought. God only gave him to me for four years. Why would He take him away from me now? Why? It didn't make sense to me. God is an awesome, wonderful God who loves Ron and loves me, and loves his mom and dad who just lost their only daughter 2 years before. Why would God put them through that? They don't deserve that pain. Ron is their baby, the one who proved doctors wrong all his life; why would this happen now? I had to believe it was going to be OK. During the waiting, my small group leader asked if Ron had life insurance. This was horribly hard to think about. But I had to.

The next few days were so hard. He wasn't improving. He wasn't waking up. He wasn't flinching when staff poked and prodded and did what they had to do. Normally, someone who had open-heart bypass surgery would be in pain. He wasn't in any pain. We knew he was in Heaven. This was just his shell hooked up to machines. We still talked to him and held his hand. I joked and tried to be silly, believing he could hear me. I believed he could hear us. I believed he could hear every one of us. The doctors told us that Sunday, 72 hours would be up and they would know if Ron was going to have any brain activity.

# OCTOBER 2, 2011

Sunday morning, a neurologist, who happens to go to our church, was there and evaluated Ron. The nurse called Ron's mom, dad, me, and my two kids in the conference room. There were already people up to visit us and Ron and they waited in the waiting room. This was so tough because the neurologist knew Ron's mom and dad. He had to choke back tears. He told us Ron's brain had gone too long without oxygen. He told us Ron would probably never regain consciousness. IF he did, it would be that of an infant. We all cried so hard. We knew we had to make that decision we didn't want to make, but knew we had to make. Ron had a living will and he clearly stated he did not want to be kept alive by machines. He wanted to go to Heaven. Machines did not mean any quality of life. In Heaven, he would have eternal life. He would not walk with a limp. His left hand, which I dearly loved, would not be bent over. He would be made new. He would be with his sister, who he dearly loved. He would be with his grandma he dearly loved, and other grandparents and loved ones. We knew he was already there. This was just his shell. We told the doctor we needed to take him off life support, but needed time to let other friends and family get here to say goodbye. We told him we would let the nurses know what time when we decided. I made calls; Ron's dad made calls. Everyone in the waiting room cried. I texted the tech director at FBC, as church was in between services. Our church had been praying for Ron. Small groups prayed; Bible study groups were praying. The Tech Arts Director told the other staff and pastors there. After church, more people came up.

My family came up, and worship leaders and some on the tech team came up.

Small group had started up the week before. We had two new couples join. Ron and I had not met them yet, but one of them brought up a huge basket of fruit. Again, we <u>OWNED</u> that ICU waiting room. I was devastated, but I knew we had to do this. My heart broke for Ron's mom and dad, who were losing two kids in two years. It just didn't feel fair. Not fair at all. But God doesn't promise us fair. I remember some family and friends in the waiting room were watching Chiefs football. Ron dearly loved the Chiefs. I went in and told Ron the Chiefs were actually ahead, that rarely happened! The nurse heard me talking to him about the Chiefs winning. She asked if I wanted her to turn on the TV for him so he can hear it. She turned it on and put the speaker by his ear. it was the last few minutes of the game. The Chiefs won. I will never forget that. I believe that Ron heard it.

The two worship leaders were there. I asked if, before Ron was disconnected, we could go in and all sing. We set the time for 8 p.m. We told the nurse what we were going to do and asked how many people we could have in his room at that time. She told us as many people as we wanted, as long as they could get to him to do what they need to do.

People came in and out of his room all day. We cried, we talked about him, different ones in the room told stories about Ron, we talked about his life. We cried some more. It didn't make sense to me. I wanted all my life to find my soul mate and God only let me have him for four years. Again, it just didn't seem fair. I couldn't understand it. But, I know God knew what He was doing, I knew I had so much support, I would be OK. The pastors and church family, my family, Ron's family, and all our friends were amazing. We were so grateful and blessed to be a part of an amazing church.

Before 8 p.m., the ones who wanted to be in Ron's room all crammed in his tiny ICU room. I bet we had 10-12, maybe more, in there. The staff were amazing. Our two worship leaders and pastor led everyone in singing "It Is Well." I sat on one side of Ron, holding his hand and crying my eyes out. Ron's mom sat on his other side, holding his hand, crying her eyes out. People sang and they sang loud. They sang, they cried, and to this day that song gets me. I can still hear them singing. I bet that whole floor could hear that song. Then, I had to go out of the room--so did the others who did not want to watch the staff do all they needed to do to take him off life support. They told us they thought he would go pretty fast afterwards. After the singing, many people went home. Some stayed. At the end, it was Ron's mom and dad, my kids, the Tech Arts Director, and me. Ron lasted longer than they thought. Staff asked if we wanted to go up to Palliative Care. We decided to, and the staff made the arrangements. Ron's dad and my son and daughter went to take some things up and to see the room. Ron's mom and tech director and I were in his room at 23:25 when he took his last breath. It was over. I remember Ron's mom said there was rejoicing in Heaven. Staff called Palliative Care and told others to come back to his room. We didn't need that room now. Staff gave me a quilt that people donate to Palliative Care. He was covered up with that when he took his last breath.

We all cried and cried. Leaving that room and that hospital was so hard. Leaving Ron was so hard. I still remember walking through the surgery waiting room and to the parking lot to the car. That was a sad walk. I felt numb, I felt sad, I felt confused why God took him from me--I felt a lot of different things. I was happy for Ron, though. He was walking with Jesus, reuniting with others gone before him. Going into the house was very difficult. I'm thankful my kids were with me. I walked in and immediately remembered the last time Ron was there, EMS, the horror of what happened in our tiny living room just a few days earlier. His last words, "call Mom and Dad first" and his last sounds of life leaving him. I can't spell those sounds, but trust me, you don't ever want to hear them, and you never want to hear them again.

While at the hospital, some people suggested I call a funeral home whose director goes to our church. We didn't know him, but he was a Christian and we decided that's who we could contact. A zillion things were going through my head, but I was so numb, dazed, and so very sad and lost. Just being back in the house was so hard. Each room had significance. Seeing anything that was his made me cry. His kitten,

Savannah Joy (Joy because she did bring him much joy, just for a short amount of time). I felt exhausted, but there was so much to do. We met with the funeral director. It just wasn't fair, not at all. But again, God doesn't promise us fair. He promises love and strength and rest and mercy and I kept having to tell myself that if He brings me to it, He will bring me through it. I am so very thankful for my family, my church family, and my friends. I cannot imagine how I could have ever gotten through it without them.

Getting back to the funeral home and arrangements. My brother brought my sister down to stay with me through all this. We all went to the funeral home with Ron's mom and dad. On the way there, I texted the Tech Arts Director at church and asked if he thought he could come up with some guys from the tech team and him to be pall-bearers. It was a matter of just a few minutes and he had names for me. Wow! Ron dearly loved serving on the tech team. So, besides Ron's brother who lives in Indiana, a nephew, Ron's brother-in-law, my son, and my brother were honorary pall-bearers. The rest were tech team. I thought he should be buried in his black tech team shirt. The tech team guys all wore their shirts. The songs, that was rough. I ran all my thoughts by Ron's mom and dad. It wasn't just my husband; it was their son, their baby. I love them dearly and wanted their input, advice, suggestions and their wishes, too. They had him 45 years. I only had him four years. I cannot even begin to imagine their pain, their loss.... again. Can't even imagine.

Going through my pics, and Ron's mom and dad going through all their years of pics, was so hard. All their memories--baby, toddler, grade school, pre-teen, teen, young adult. 45 years of pics. It was hard going through my pics of him. We didn't have a lot of time. The Tech Arts Director needed them and music to do his magic and make the video. We all met, sorted through pics, cried, laughed...some of those pics were funny looking!!!! The one song on the video was Jesus Messiah. Our worship team sang that at the last Overflow we went to the night before his surgery. His last time also serving on tech team was that weekend. He got to train in the Worship Center where services are held. He always served with kids. He loved serving and was so happy to get to learn on the big equipment. He even brought home homework.

Those next few days were crazy busy, yet seemed like slow motion. Our small group brought food. Amazing food! My sister stayed with me. My two kids were there, too. Wow, getting ready for my husband's funeral. He was only 45 years old. It just didn't feel fair.

The day came for his viewing. He was in state from noon to 4 at the funeral home. It just didn't seem real. Just like seeing others in a coffin, it looked like he was breathing. The funeral home did an awesome job on him. He made him grin a little, just like Ron would grin. How did he know that? My daughter and I went there alone. It was nice to have time without others swarming around. I knew that would change that evening when he would be at church for visitation. Flowers were pretty, video and music perfect, although it made me cry. Everything made me cry.

That evening when we went to visitation at church really got me. I didn't know it, but he was downstairs in the room he loved to serve in. Now someone else was at the booth doing video, lights and sound. His video was playing on the screens where he had words to songs for kids to sing. He was there, one last time, in the room he loved. I took his Bible and the Heaven book he was reading to me. I took his bowling trophies, his weight lifting trophies, and his huge belt buckle he won weight lifting.

Yeah, the man with his left hand shaped differently lifted weights in high school. Like I said, no one could tell him he couldn't do something! <u>HE</u> had to try and try and maybe do it differently and <u>HE</u> would decide if he could or could not do something. I wish I had that much guts.

The Tech Arts Director had given Ron's mom and dad and me a black and white picture of Ron that he took at church when he was learning his new camera. That picture was such a precious gift! It is sitting on his dresser. It's the first thing I see every morning, the last thing I look at every night. Who would have known when he took that pic that it would become so precious to us.

Back to visitation. There were so many people there! Lots of people I didn't know, but people who knew Ron and/or his mom and dad. I was so blown away by all the compassion from people who I didn't know, people I had not known very long, and people who were friends and loved ones. His cousin and nephew got into town from Iowa and came straight to visitation. She was his favorite cousin. He loved her very much. I could tell she was heartbroken.

I cried and cried during that visitation. Just seeing all the people. My friends, my family, my church family. It was so overwhelming and so amazing.

The pastors and staff were so comforting. I cannot imagine going through this time without them and my church family. My family and I did not have any of this when my father passed in 1998 and when my mother passed in 2009. They couldn't find a church they felt welcomed in, a part of, or like they belonged to, so they didn't go. Man, those times would have been much easier if there were people to support us.

October 6 at 10 a.m. was his funeral. No one in my family does mornings very well, and four people trying to get ready at the last minute with one bathroom was a trip. My son was a casket bearer and wanted to wear his Army uniform, especially since Ron's brother was also a casket bearer and retired from the Army. We were running late and his button popped off. Great. We didn't have time to wait for him to change or to fix the button. He was upset that wearing his uniform without a button would make him out of uniform. He wasn't going to go. I was devastated. It was getting late--I didn't want to leave him and have him miss this. We had to go. When we got to church, I told Ron's brother, my brother, and a good friend who was like a mentor to my son. They all worked their magic and somehow got him there. No one cared that he was technically out of uniform. Meanwhile, while that was going on, all the emotions, all the people, all the hugs from family, friends, church family, people I didn't know. Talk about overwhelming. That was just the lobby! Oh, yeah, going in the Worship Center, I saw my cousin! I hugged him and told him he looked old! Yep, that's me. Sometimes, whatever pops in my head pops right out of my mouth! I had seen him a year or so before at his mother's funeral. More on that in a minute. Inside, Ron's casket was placed right by the tech booth. Well, that did it!!! I cried like a baby. He was where he loved, one last time. In his tech arts shirt, with 4 casket bearers from the tech team wearing their tech arts shirts. What an honor. What a way to honor Ron.

I was amazed at the people there. I should not have been though; this is an awesome church. Tuesday morning Bible study started up for Fall and were meeting downstairs. People were working hard in the kitchen preparing the meal. It was time to begin. Deep breath -- many of them. Kleenex – a whole box!!!

A friend who plays the Native American flute started off by playing

"Amazing Grace." Yep, that did it. It was so beautiful, so haunting, so perfect. Ron and I always cried when the worship team played that song. Now it's just me. Man, that was hard.

And the pastor, what can I say? He was one of the first to be with us that awful day when everything went very wrong, very fast. He was with us, waiting and praying, hugging, supporting, making me laugh and cry. He was with us so much through this. He experienced this with us. He knew Ron, he knew his strengths and weaknesses. He knew we weren't perfect, but he knew Ron's faith and Ron's love for serving. He knew Ron's love for God. I remember he told us at the hospital that the Sunday before his surgery he wanted to pray over him. He said Ron said "Guys, I'm okay, and if anything happens, I know where I'm going." He was in the ICU room with the others when they sang It Is Well. He was there when they unhooked him from life support. He called me several mornings after Ron passed to check on me. He knew Ron; he didn't have to rely on what people told him about Ron.

I remember he asked how many people there were in a small group. He talked about how Ron's mom and dad's and my small group were there for us, how we owned that surgery waiting room and ICU waiting room. He talked about salvation. He talked about how Ron finally found a place where he fit in and was accepted instead of made fun of. He talked about how Ron was determined and didn't give up because of his disability. He talked about the awards he won for weight lifting. And he read Ron's last entry in his L-3 Journal that day. Ron always gave God his first and his best, not his last and leftovers.

I have to include what Ron wrote. It just needs to be told. I'm sure he won't care. Ron was a very private person, but I'm sure he's okay with sharing this. I can see his grin, his smile and rolling his eyes and shaking his head like he always did. I miss that smile, those rolling eyes and shaking his head. I loved making him laugh and coming up with off-the-wall stuff. It's serious. It's from his heart, it's his last prayer to the God he loved. I'm so happy my pastor shared it at his service. I feel I need to share it with whoever reads this.

## 9/29/11 JOHN 7:37-38

R: "On the last and greatest day of the feast, Jesus stood and said in a loud voice, "If anyone is thirsty, let him come to me and drink. Whoever believes in me as the scripture has said, streams of living water will flow from within him."

E: Jesus is knowingly testing the people. He makes this statement knowing that His spirit cannot be given because His time has yet to come but in making this statement He creates talk and thought among the people, the result of which some believe, some think He is the prophet, others questioned how He could be the Christ because of His origin. The people were divided but no one touched Him.

A: Be confident when talking about Jesus. Help others to understand that Jesus is the Son of man; He can be believed in.

P: Dear Jesus, You created a perfect world for man to dwell in, but man fell into sin. You sent Your one and only Son to redeem man, but He was rejected as well. Father, mankind does not deserve You. I do not deserve You and yet You freely give of Yourself, thank You. Thank You for all You have done and for Your love. Amen.

Ron's last entry in his L-3 Journal, his last prayer.

I'm sure when the pastor read this others were crying with me.

One of our other pastors talked about Ron. His brother got up and talked. Man, he was brave. A good friend, who was my son's mentor, talked. They all made me cry.

And then there were the songs. Our group leader sang "Great Is Thy Faithfulness"…yeah, that got me. Then "Hallelujah to My King" by the Overflow worship leader. Her voice is that of an angel. She sang the very first time I went to this church with Ron. She sang at our reception when Ron and I repeated our vows, so my son could give me away since he was in Iraq when we got married. I still cry whenever I hear her voice. And then, the song that forever will be in my head and heart, along with that picture of that day when so many people crammed in that tiny ICU room and sang. Yep, it only seemed right to have our worship leader play his guitar and sing "It Is Well!" It's been almost two years now and I can't get through that song without hearing them all sing and seeing Ron in that bed, hooked up to every machine imaginable but not saving him. But Ron was saved, saved by his loving God. Then a "Prayer Song" on Native American Flute. That haunting, beautiful sound. It goes right to your soul.

After that is such a blur. Pastor escorted me out of the Worship Center, crying my eyes out. The ride to the cemetery wasn't far, but it seemed like it took forever. I don't remember much, except it was windy. Under a tree. A plot that his mom and dad bought for them someday. Doesn't seem fair their baby boy needed it first. It's a beautiful cemetery. It was a short service there. I remember taking flowers from the casket spray. It's all a fog. So many people. So many hugs, so many tears, so many thoughts, prayers and so much love. It was all amazing, yet heartbreaking. Family came from Indianapolis, Vegas, Iowa, Missouri, and here in Kansas. I'm still in awe at all the people. I know Ron didn't feel that that many people loved him. He would have been humbled.

Some people had other commitments and had to leave; others went back to church for lunch. It was so very hard being in that room, eating without Ron. When he would serve, we would eat supper at church between services. It didn't feel right being there without him. It's still hard being any place in church without him. Walking past the room where he served, where the night before, he was in there for the last time. His video on the screens. It's just too much to handle. It's so hard. Lunch was awesome. Remember my cousin I said looked older? Well, silly me! We were going through the lunch line and he stated he lived close by and he and his wife watched this church being built. Really? Then at the table, he talked about going to KU. KU? That wasn't him!!! My kissing cousin went to K-State!! Wow, another BAM moment! He wasn't my kissing cousin I wanted to marry when we were younger! Never could understand why I couldn't marry him!!! It wasn't my cousin, but his older brother. I love him, but boy did I feel stupid. Yep, I embarrassed myself good, right off the bat. Lunch was amazing, as always, when they serve any meal. I saw some friends of ours who were volunteering to do this lunch. Ron loved them. So of course I cried, again. People were visiting, laughing, crying, hugging. Eventually, it was over. Time to say bye, thanks, more hugs, more tears. Time to load flowers in the car and divide them up between Ron's mom and dad. My place was very small.

I remember going back in that house. It felt weird. All the craziness of preparing for the visitation and funeral was over. I am very thankful for my family staying with me. Me and my three big dogs, my son's German Shepherd, and Ron's cat. The animals outnumbered people 5-4. It's OK, cause my animals were my therapy, my companions. My calm, my laughter, my stress and my need. I could not imagine life without them.

In the next few days, I remembered bills needed to be paid. Ron always did that. I found the ledger where he always kept track of what and who he paid. I found, on top of the ledger, a new ledger. I opened it and started crying. It's just like he knew I would need it. The other one wasn't used up yet, but he started a new one. He wrote out Oct., Nov., and Dec. He wrote who needed paid, how much and when. I cried and cried. He knew. He knew. He followed Dave Ramsey's Financial Peace Program. I looked in the checkbook. There was some money. Not a lot, but some. He had money in savings, just like Dave says to do. He knew I would need it. Then I saw the address labels and checks. Both our names were on them. That very quiet, sad moment when it hit me. I would have to get new ones, with just my name. It was too much to bear. Something so simple as address labels and checks could make me lose it. Then I remembered getting in the car that Sunday night, leaving the hospital. It was spotless. I remembered that very hot day before his surgery. He loved the heat. He spent all day washing and waxing the outside of the car. He washed windows, inside and out, he vacuumed, he used Armour All, all inside. He took pride in his work. I remember him saying his dad told him if he was gonna do something, to do it right. He was very meticulous. I took him tea and begged him to take a break. It's like he knew. That car was spotless. It needs cleaned again--I wish he was here to clean it again!

Something else that I remembered is another day before his surgery. He sat on the front step, on another hot day, and spent all day cleaning every tool in his tool box. Again, being very meticulous. Again, it's like he knew. He also had changed the cat litter. It was his kitten. He always changed it. Now I was going to have to. I didn't, and still don't, like that much. I always tell him I really wish he was here to do this cat litter thing! He knew. I know he knew. It's like he was preparing me to be without him. It's been almost two years and I still miss him terribly.

A new normal. That's what remember my pastor told me I needed to find. I made appointments a few times to cry. The holidays were coming up and I knew they were gonna be hard. Hmmm...a new normal. I have never been normal before!

Thanksgiving was hard. I don't remember much about it, except it was horribly hard. Christmas. Ron dearly loved Christmas. I ordered the book Heaven by Randy Alcorn and passed them out to family at Christmas, and to pastors and staff at church. Along with the poem about Christmas in Heaven. I need to share this poem, too. It made us all cry. I need to share the tears. I rolled each one in a scroll and tied it with burgundy ribbon. Burgundy was Ron's favorite color. Here is a section of that poem

## My First Christmas in Heaven
### Wanda Bencke

I Know How Much You Miss Me. I See The Pain Inside Your Heart,
But I Am Not So Far Away. We Really Aren't Apart.
So Be Happy For Me Dear Ones. You Know I hold you Dear,
And Be Glad I'm Spending Christmas With Jesus Christ This Year.

# My Small Group

After all the services and things calmed down, I tried to discover a "new normal." Sometimes I did OK; other times I'd break down just seeing something of Ron's. Small group brought food for over a week. What a blessing to someone who doesn't like to cook! It took a little while to get brave enough to go to Tuesday morning Bible study again. I only knew one person at my table, the Tech Arts Director's wife. I found out one lady, who was older than I am, had been a widow for about a year. Wow, God was amazing!!! My table leader was amazing, very supportive. She would somehow know when I was down, or not wanting to go to Bible study, cause she would text me out of the blue and ask how I was doing! God at work again! She was so encouraging! One woman lost her son to murder during this time. One woman would later become my Herbalife sponsor and nutrition coach. Almost two years later, two of the women at my table would become my Herbalife down line. But, more importantly, my friend who was the widow, opened her beautiful home for a new women's small group. One woman who was also at that table became a co-leader in this new small group. Who knew that from those women at that table that three of them would become friends I would see on a regular basis after that Tuesday morning Bible study. God knew. He knew and He blows my mind how He picks people and puts them in my life!!

During this time, my Monday night small group that Ron and I belonged to, was super supportive. Two new families had joined. After one evening, they gave me a wire basket with a Fall-colored napkin, with some cocoa packets and other comforting items. The most important thing in that basket was Jesus Calling. A daily devotional that I still read every morning. These two didn't know me, but they reached out to me, and they will never know how much that meant to me.

Going to small group was very difficult. Just the drive there was heart-wrenching. Ron wasn't with me. He always drove there. Now I had to drive, alone and crying all the way most of the time. Inside the house where Ron and I went for the last three years was equally, if not more, difficult. I loved the people there, my leaders, the others in the group. Some had stopped coming because of very important obligations. I dearly missed them. New people joined. But now they were all couples. I wasn't a couple anymore. Being in that beautiful house with awesome, supportive people was so painful. Being there without Ron with me was more than I could handle. Sometimes I just couldn't make myself go. With the drive there, and being in the house without him, broke my heart. When we would leave, Ron and I usually discussed what we learned or how people needed our prayers. So, I usually cried all the way back home, without him.

All that summer I struggled with the decision to stay in this familiar group, who had been there for me through this devastating time in my life. Should I just suck it up and keep going? Would it ever get easier? Or should I branch out and be brave and join a new small group? One for women. None of that couples stuff. But what if I didn't connect? What if I didn't feel like I belonged? What if I didn't know anyone? Would anyone understand my grief? My journey? I debated back and forth all summer. I had talked to the small group coordinator about where I would fit in. I wasn't comfortable joining a group already connected, already meshed and me be the new girl. I found out that my friend who is a widow offered her home to meet in; the other woman from Tuesday morning was going to be a co-leader. Wow! A new women's group, with two people I already knew! I decided to try it. The small group coordinator, who I knew, was going to help us get started and then leave our group, since she and her husband host their own small group. Well, I discovered that these women were awesome!

God, again, hand-picked them and put them in my life! We are very diverse. Some have been divorced like me; some are single parents like I was. Most have experienced loss of loved ones, and would experience loss during our first year. Wow!!! We are different ages, with different issues, different pasts, hurts, hopes and dreams. But we meshed and we meshed fast! Oh, yeah, the small group coordinator? She loves us so much she stayed! I am so blessed by these women. God is amazing!

I miss my first small group. Especially during Sharefest, a yearly thing our church partners with other churches to help show God's love by painting playgrounds, railings, parking lot lines, cleaning up landscape, planting new bushes or plants and just beautifying schools who need our help. Ron and I loved Sharefest. He was usually in charge of pouring paint. Since I am not physically able to do the work, I sat at the registration table and told people to find guys in red shirts and they would tell them what to do. I always sat at this table with a friend from small group and her mother, before she went to Heaven. I loved those times. Now, I wasn't in that small group. I was so lost that day. I didn't know others at that table. I felt left out, sad, and I wanted Ron back. Someone else was pouring paint. My friends weren't there. One of my friends from the new small group met me there. It was her first Sharefest. I was happy she was there. But, Ron wasn't there. I know this year will be hard, too. But, hopefully, women from my new small group will be there.

Besides Tuesday morning Bible study, that Spring I went to Griefshare Group through Finding Hope. My leader was also a Tech Arts Director volunteer who Ron had trained in the children's program. This group was very small, which I was happy for. Remember the one I said lost her son to murder? She and her husband were there. I needed to deal with the loss of Ron, but also the loss of my mother. The hardest part of Finding Hope was that all the groups met in the children's theater. The room where Ron served. Where I would hang out with him during the second service, where his visitation was. That was horribly hard to even walk past the door to that room, let alone go inside. Sometimes I just wasn't strong enough to go in. Sometimes I didn't go. I knew I needed to, and felt better when I did go. Griefshare really helped and I highly recommend it to anyone dealing with the loss of a loved one--whether it be a spouse, parent, child, sibling, anyone.

I really needed Finding Hope. When Griefshare ended and Finding Hope started up again, I took Boundaries. Boy, did I need that one! Group was larger, leaders were awesome. A good friend was also in group, so I didn't feel so out of place. I made another friend at that group. I admit I didn't always do my homework or go to group. I realized I needed to be around people, and who better to be around than people also needing Finding Hope? After that group, I was excited to meet other parents or family members at a new group being offered – a group for family members dealing with loved ones with PTSD. Sadly, that first night, no one showed up for that group, or the group for people experiencing PTSD. The awesome pastor who is in charge of Finding Hope suggested I go to Anger Group. I went, but felt out of place since I am all about peace and love, not anger. It was a small group which I liked. I made a friend, and became friends with our group leader. God is so good! She understands PTSD and helps veterans and wrote the book and study guide for this Anger Group. Do you see how God was working? I don't have an anger problem, but I met an awesome friend who is an author!!! Remember in the beginning when someone in the Summer Finding Hope group "Life's Healing Choices" mentioned I write this book and I said "I know an author?"!!! Wow, it really amazes me how He is constantly putting people in my life.

Between Finding Hope, Tuesday morning Bible study and small group—they have been a huge lifeline to me. Breaks are hard, but sometimes we meet during breaks just to keep in touch and give/get support.

## My Move

Since Ron's passing, and no longer having his income, I knew I was gonna have to move. I didn't want to, but disability isn't much to live on. I tried finding a part-time job, but no luck. Staying in our house for almost a year had its ups and downs. I would look out the window and wait for Ron to drive up. Then remembering that wasn't ever going to happen. Our room, the room where he had his computer desk and did the bills and budget, the living room where we would sit and talk, dream, discuss stuff, cry, veg, watch TV or listen to his stereo, all were too painful. Also, the kitchen where he would cook was difficult. I hate to cook. He loved to cook and clean. I would look at the kitchen and wish he were in it cooking cause I got hungry! He taught me a lot about a lot of things. Some things I remember and use, some things never made sense to me anyway. Remember, I'm a dreamer. Practical people and practical, logical stuff don't make sense to me!

But I kinda had to be practical. Life wasn't easy. My kids and family helped any way they could. Ron's niece, husband and boys mowed the yard–gave me the family discount–free, just cookies and strawberry milk for them when they were done. That helped a lot. Still, it was hard being in that same house. It was also hard to leave. My sister had spent a lot of time and hard work helping me paint a couple of rooms and the hallway before I decided to move. Oh, well, it needed it anyway.

I looked and looked for a place to live. A place I could afford and in an area that was safe to live in alone. And a place where I could have my three big dogs, a little dog, and Ron's cat. That place either didn't exist or I couldn't find it or afford it. I wanted to be outside of town, in the country, or in one of the small towns close. I needed and wanted to be close to my son, Ron's mom and dad, and church. Nothing. Couldn't find any place that would work. I broke down and looked at apartments. The ones I could afford were in parts of town I didn't feel safe in alone. The ones I liked, or would settle for, either didn't allow pets or were too expensive. After searching awhile, I remembered Ron talking about townhomes where he lived when he turned 18, his first place. I looked them up on the internet. I knew someone who lived there and loved it. I remember driving through there. I finally went in the office and asked for info. I remember asking about pets. I was told dogs had to be small, a certain weight limit. I remember crying to the receptionist, telling her my husband passed away and I had four dogs, one of them was a small Chocolate Lab that he gave me before he passed away. I left the office in tears. The thought of losing Jake, Dakota and Sophie broke my heart.

Sophie has such a gentle spirit. I found her on Craigslist. Told ya I was a Craigslist Junkie! I saw her picture. She was only two years old, was free, spayed, housebroken–everything I wanted. I showed Ron her pic. He kept telling me we already had Jake and Dakota and his kitten, Savannah. I kept on, pleading my case–she needed a home and we had a home. Ron finally gave in. Poor guy! I was so bad. I felt a connection to her just from her pic, but all I have to do is look into a dog's eyes and I'm hooked. I called the people and they lived in Leavenworth. Ron wasn't too thrilled, but we drove there and got her. He kept reminding me she wasn't free if we had to drive to get her. She was already spayed and it didn't cost to get her except for the drive, so I didn't get it!

Poor Ron, not a dog person, and now had three big dogs living with him, plus my son's German Shepherd visited to play a lot.

Sophie was lovable and well-behaved. I think she might have started to grow on him. We only had her a month, I think, before his surgery.

Back to moving. I don't remember how or when I found out that since I am on disability, Sophie could be my companion dog since she brought me comfort and helped me deal with stuff. That was a huge relief. I filled out paperwork and did all I was supposed to do. There was only one townhome available. I looked at it, and had Ron's mom and dad look at it. I respect their opinion and wanted their input. Man, this place is so small. And steps. I hate steps. Steps upstairs to two bedrooms. Steps downstairs to the basement and washer and dryer. I liked the idea of finally having a basement with this crazy, unpredictable Kansas weather! It had carpet. Vacuuming is painful. Ron always vacuumed. Steps are good exercise, but on bad fibro days would be very difficult. Downsizing big time! Not enough room for all my years of stuff I acquired through the years. Didn't have the energy or time for a garage sale, so I donated tons of stuff to the VA. Many people don't think about our vets and how some are in need of basic house stuff. I had stuff, so I gave a lot to the VA.

My biggest problem? Jake and Dakota. Jake was now almost 7, Dakota almost 8. I had them longer than any animal–ever. They kept me company when my son was in Iraq. Even though they were huge babies, just Jake's size would intimidate anyone from breaking in while living in Manhattan and here. They ate a lot, but I loved them so much. Dakota was such a goofball! He was such a routine dog. Anything out of his routine or anything moved or new and he wouldn't know what to do. He was afraid of his own shadow. He made me laugh. He loved the snow. He would dive nose first into the snow and flop around like a fish! I called them Dakota angels. Even if there was just a dusting, he loved it. The thought of not having him and his hair around anymore broke my heart. And Jake, my miniature horse! He was 110 pounds of spoiled rotten dog! He barked at everything, but he was a sweetheart. Both were very loyal and faithful dogs. I went to my pastor and asked if he knew someone who would want them. I prayed someone from church would take them. Someone I could trust to take good care of them, to make them part of their family. One family wanted only Dakota. I was told they would be the best people for them, that they were awesome people and would love him. But what about Jake? I couldn't separate them. I just couldn't do it. They grew up together. I kept looking. A family from my old small group considered it, but it didn't work out. I refused to put an ad on Craigslist, even though I had gotten Sophie, Sampson and Lucky from there. Sampson only lasted a week. He was awesome to me, but didn't like my other dogs. He was a Saint Bernard. His owner was being deployed. Just like Sophie's family. He turned my house upside down. I found him an awesome home in the country. That was only a few months after Ron passed away.

I couldn't put an ad out for them because I was afraid someone wouldn't keep them together. That they would sell them or something bad would happen. I just had a bad feeling. I asked everybody. A friend made flyers for me to put up at vets. Nothing. I called rescues. They were all full. One rescue lady yelled at me and asked if everyone was moving to some town that didn't allow dogs? I cried like a baby and hung up on her. I never do that. It's not a Christian thing to do, but I was running out of time. I was tired of packing and moving stuff to the new place. I was tired of being tired. I didn't want to get rid of them. I had to. I ran out of options. I had such a hard time dealing with the thought of not having them anymore. I'd been though a lot with Jake and Dakota. I loved them dearly. I was running out of rescues to call. I refused to take them to the shelter here. It's a kill shelter. Owner surrender costs money. I didn't have it. I was told by many people that surrendered animals are the first to be put to sleep. No, killed. Killed because I couldn't keep them. That wasn't fair and I was determined that was NOT going to happen to them. They were awesome dogs and didn't deserve to be killed.

I remembered that someone who worked in my financial advisor's office had told me about her love of animals. I called her. She was happy to help and she spent many hours helping me find someone. She put me in touch with a lady who works at a shelter in a different county. She also helped call contacts she dealt with. She talked to Retriever Rescue of Colorado. There was finally some hope! Time was running out. I had to be out of the house in a few days. I talked to this rescue. She put out an emergency call for foster homes for Jake and Dakota. I was told there wasn't a foster home that could take both. I cried so hard. I felt horrible they had to be separated. I felt like a very bad dog mom. But my choices were limited. This rescue--who promised to take care of them--they do home inspections and interviews of people wanting to adopt them and they charge. They charge a lot, so people have to really want them. There were many calls between the lady at the shelter helping me and the rescue. We finally had a day and a time to meet so some transporters could take Jake and Dakota to Kansas City, to a place I forgot the name of (sounded like a truck stop for animals). This place would keep Jake and Dakota till another transporter could drive them from Kansas City to the rescue in Colorado. From there, they would be taken to their separate foster homes. Makes me cry to just write this. It's been almost a year now and I still miss them like crazy. My heart hurts, remembering that day, and missing them every day since. I admit it. I'm a wimp. I'm a cry baby. I cry so easily, especially thinking about my big puppies. That dreaded morning came when I loaded up Jake and Dakota and their bowls and crates. I was donating bowls and crates to the lady and shelter that helped me. I didn't need them anymore. Sophie and Lucky had their bowls and crates.

I went to the vet parking lot where I was told to go. The lady from the shelter was there. I gave her Jake's and Dakota's vet records, filled out paperwork, and signed them away. I felt like I was giving up rights to my kids. I couldn't know where they are and couldn't ever try to get them back. Crying the whole time I was signing them away, broke my heart. I was told we needed to wait for the transporters to get there. A van from the shelter was waiting for the transporters to take animals from them to a shelter in Salina. I was amazed at all the crates of puppies and dogs that transporters put in the other van. It was awesome that people give of their time to drive animals to a place where they can have a good home, a good life, and not be killed because they are homeless and not by their own fault.

The dogs were all taken out of the Kansas City transporter's van. It was time to load Jake and Dakota. The lady from the shelter told the transporters my story and how proud she was of me for refusing to give them to just anyone or to dump them or to take them to the kill shelter. How she knew how painful this was for me. So, of course, I cried again. Everyone wanted pics of me with Jake and Dakota one last time. That was a trip cause, of course, Jake had to bark at them the whole time. Then they had me put Jake and Dakota in the van going to Kansas City. I can still see their faces as I squeezed them as tight as I could and just sobbed. I'm sobbing writing this. Like I said, I'm a wimp.

I remember not wanting to let go of them. I remember thinking, I wasn't ever going to see them again. The transporters and shelter lady gave me time with them. But, hey, I could have taken all day, if they would have let me. It was time for them to go. They all had schedules and things to do, other animals to take care of. I remember sitting in my car crying like crazy, trying to collect myself so I could drive home. It still seems like it was yesterday. I was told I could email the rescue and find out how they were and if they had been adopted. I could have pics of them but could never see them in person or try to get them back. I'd give anything to have them back. Anything. I emailed the rescue several times. I always got an answer. The last one was November, 2012. It said "I know you miss your boys very much. I will pass on any information I receive regarding their adoptions to you." Yes, I kept that message. I never received anything about them being adopted. I don't know if they are still in foster homes or if they have been adopted. I just haven't been told. I am so very thankful for this rescue. These people are animal lovers who open their homes and hearts to homeless animals and keep them until they have a forever home. I wish their forever home was with me. Whenever I see a Golden Retriever or Black Lab, I think of them. They were still together the last time I saw them. On their way to a new life, a new adventure, a new journey without me. I love them so much.

At least, I still have Sophie and Lucky. I told you Sophie's story. Now about Lucky...

My sister wanted a little dog. Where she lives has size restrictions, too. Being the Craigslist Junkie that I was, I found a dog I thought my sister would like. I talked to the people who had Lucky and to my sister. Lucky was free. I always had big dogs--never ever thought I would want a little dog. When I went to pick up Lucky, when I walked in the door, she practically jumped in my arms. She was spunky, she was adorable, and she was spoiled! I was told her story how she showed up at these people's house one day. They put out ads in the newspaper, flyers in the neighborhood, in the vet's, all over trying to find her owner. These people already had a couple of dogs and kids and couldn't keep her. I was given the sweater they bought her besides the one she was wearing, her bowls, and leash. Well, this dog had totally won my heart. Driving the hour to my sister's house was a challenge since this dog insisted on being in my lap! I wasn't used to a dog riding in my lap. My dogs were all big dogs and sat in the back where they belonged!

I really kinda liked this little dog and drove slower than usual to my sister's house. She thought she was cute. My brother and I took her to the vet there. No microchip. Was told little dogs can have allergy problems, to not give her any wheat or grains. I could tell this dog was not gonna be cheap! My sister and I took her to the pet store where I bought her a small kennel, a soft pink bed, a pink collar and matching leash. Apparently this dog had been to a pet store before, because she knew the toy aisle! It was hilarious! She would jump up and try to get toys. We got her a squeaky toy. Yep, this dog was already spoiled and I had a feeling it was just the beginning!

The people said they named her Lucky cause she was lucky she didn't get hit by a car, cause they lived by two very busy streets. The next day or so, my sister called me and was frantic. Lucky had bolted out the front door and ran away. People helped her look; even the police helped. It was December and it was cold. They almost got her and she would bolt. She was fast. They looked and looked and couldn't find her. My sister was worried all night since it was cold and Lucky had crossed the highway when she ran. That next morning, my sister saw Lucky running around her complex. So, she had crossed back over the highway safely. She was Lucky! My sister finally caught her and called and wanted me to come get her. She couldn't handle this dog being so fast and was afraid she would bolt out the door again and maybe not be so lucky. So, I went and got her. I had Jake, Dakota, Sophie, and Savannah (Ron's kitten). Yes, I'm a crazy dog lady. She has personality; she has silliness about her. The vet said he thought she was 3 or 4 years old. I decided to keep her.

She immediately thought she ruled the house! Potty training her was a hassle, but she finally got the hang of it. The big dogs had a big back yard to run around and play in. I couldn't let Lucky out there--she is white and the back was largely dirt. She wouldn't be white for long. I also read that her breed, West Highland Terrier, loves to dig and to chase squirrels, and to escape. She did escape many times. She bolted out the front door many times. I would go out after her. It became a game. I would almost get her and she would take off again. I lived by two busy streets and she was lucky she never ran to them or got hit. Sometimes my fibromyalgia would be so bad I could barely walk, but I would hobble down the street, around the block or blocks, till I got her. Sometimes other people would see her and catch her for me.

I always thought people who dressed their dogs were crazy. Well, I know I'm crazy. Lucky loved wearing her sweaters. I would buy them on sale and she would get all excited. I would hold up two of them and she would jump up and touch the one she wanted. Lucky isn't stupid. Lucky IS spoiled. I lovingly call her my diva dog! She loves to be pampered. She kept me busy, so that helped. I walked her and we bonded in a much different way than I did with my other dogs. She was special. Her name was Lucky, but I was the one who was lucky. I really didn't like that name much. I was told if I changed it – it needed to end sounding like Lucky since that's what she was used to. I couldn't think of a name I liked with the right ending, so I kept it Lucky.

I knew Ron would NOT be happy that I now had <u>four</u> dogs and his kitten. If I had the money and the land, I would have more. After Sampson and Sophie (both being dogs that had to be given up due to owners having to be deployed), I really wish I could keep dogs for people while they are deployed so they can have them back when they return. I figure if someone can give up so much to serve their country, the least I can do would be to take care of their four-legged friend. But, that hasn't happened. Maybe someday. It would be a way for me to give back to those who serve, a way to say thank you.

Ok, I rambled big time. Dogs make me do that. Back to moving. My sister helped me pack and move stuff, little by little, to the new place. We spent so many hours and so many late nights moving stuff and cleaning the old house. It was August and it was hot!!!! My sister-in-law had to be hospitalized, so my sister was needed to visit her, too. My poor sister. We can always depend on her!

The amazing moving story, though, is that a friend of mine is friends with one of the pastors at church. She knew I needed help moving big stuff. They ride motorcycles with other people and because they have bikes, they have trailers. She told me they like to help people move! I only knew my friend and my pastor, but that morning, if I remember right, about 8-12 people from their group showed up to help move big stuff. A couple and kids from my small group showed up to help and three of my small group leaders' kids showed up! I was totally amazed. And, of course, my awesome father-in-law showed up. Bless his heart. I love that man! These people from the motorcycle group came in and walked out with stuff and loaded it up so fast! I told this one guy the cat condo was heavy--he picked it up and walked out with it like it was nothing! I will never forget that! Those people, almost all of them strangers, loaded up my stuff, drove across town, and unloaded it in TWO HOURS!!! Is that amazing or what? My sister and son and I had been up all night working to get done and be ready for them bright and early. God is so amazing, that these people would give up their Saturday morning to help me move. I have to admit, I don't remember the names of all the people from that group, but I will not forget what they did for me.

I was so tired I was stupid! I was on the greeting team that month. I remember my pastor told me to get some sleep, to <u>NOT</u> go to service. I remember telling him I never had a pastor tell me not to go to church!

## Widowed Too Soon

I found this group and called about it. It's through a local hospice. I found three widow groups. Two are through two different hospices. One is a group that just meets on its own for a social brunch once a month, then at Pizza Hut once a month to celebrate birthdays. I called about all of them. One group cost money. I may still check them out, but haven't decided for sure or not. The one that is just a social one, I have a feeling I'm the youngest. The lady I talked to on the phone was very sweet. I might check them out. The one I have been to twice so far is a group called Widowed Too Soon, for people whose spouses have passed before retirement age. Last week was the first night it started back up. It goes six weeks on, six weeks off. If I remember right, there were seven women and three men last week. There were two other new ones besides me, a male and female who both lost their spouses a few months ago. Also, if I remember right, most of the others are around the two-year mark, like I am close to--October 2, 2011, the worst day of my life.

We were asked to go around the room and introduce ourselves, say our spouse's name, how long we were married, how long they have been gone, and what happened to them. Boy, was that tough! I was second to the last one to talk. By the time it was my turn, I was crying from hearing the others' stories. Good thing there is lots of boxes of Kleenex!! All I could get out was my name, Ron's name, and that we only got four years and that I waited forever to find him. That's it. That's all I could say till I broke down. I enjoyed the group. The leader has such an amazing, calm, comforting voice. After we all talked, we were given a handout called "The Terrain of the Active Grieving Process." It really makes sense. It shows how we start out with life as it was.

First – Impact: Experiencing the unthinkable. Second – Crisis: Stumbling in the dark. Third – Observation: Linking past to present – such as going through belongings, looking at pictures of spouse again, etc. Fourth – The Turn: Turning into the Wind – embracing the present, able to think about the future without spouse in it, and a future with a meaning and a purpose. Fifth – Reconstruction: Picking up the pieces – doing something different, trying to put life back together – finding joy and meaning again. Sixth – Working Through: Finding Solid Ground – grief can be like quicksand sometimes and dead-ends, have to try over and over on this path. Not a straight line from #1 to #7. Have twists, turns, caves to hide in, bumps, hills, valleys. Not all stages. Can go from one to another and back to beginning many times. Last one, Seven – Integration: Daylight.

Life in a "new normal." Life is good again, but never the same. This handout is by Elizabeth Harper Neeld, PhD. Seven Choices: Finding Daylight After Loss Shatters Your World. Like I said, this map makes sense, a lot of sense.

Last night was week #2. It went better. I got my story out. I seem to be stuck on only having had four years. The others had longer, much longer. Some were high school sweethearts who grew up together. Some had 40 years or longer, I think everyone had at least 10-12 years or more. I feel ripped off. I'm not mad at God about it. I don't want to sound, or become, bitter either. I'm at the stage where I just don't understand why God took him from me. I'm not questioning God's decision, I'm just trying to understand it. I do understand that God totally used Ron to bring me here, to a town I didn't wanna live in, to put people in place around me and to be involved in church, but most of all, to re-introduce me to Jesus again. But much more, to learn about and want to pursue a relationship with Jesus. It's not about a religion. It's about a relationship. Why Ron? Why me? Only God knows that reason. All I know is I'm very grateful. I'm not happy I had and have to go through this. I'm not happy Ron beat me to Heaven!!! But, I understand and believe God is now using me somehow, to help me and teach me how to tell my story. To use my pain to help others who are going through this. Maybe this is why I'm at this group. I'm sure I'm supposed to open my eyes, ears, and heart and learn something from someone, to maybe even make a friend, and it would be totally awesome to somehow touch someone in this group. We will see. Four more weeks, then a six-week break. I'm not big on breaks. My Tuesday morning Bible study, Tuesday night Finding Hope, small group, and now this group all take breaks. I need people. I need my church family. Breaks, especially around holidays, are hard. That's when I need people the most. Last night, after we all told our stories again, our leader read a bit from a book called Love Letters. A book of letters a guy wrote to his wife in helping him with his grief. I'm sure they help others too, as I pray somehow this book helps someone, somewhere, sometime.

This story is about the husband carrying out his wife's wishes for her cremated remains to be scattered. He scatters them in Spring Creek, Wisconsin. It was a good letter about cremation and how some people have trouble not having a marker to go to, not having a place to go pay respects to. But, it's also about how it really is about "ashes to ashes, dust to dust." It's a cycle. It makes sense. I never really thought seriously about being cremated. I've had uncles cremated, but no close family member. I'm terrified of fire, so the thought of being burned scares me. But, I'm a wimp and know I won't feel anything. It just scares me for some reason. Maybe I will learn more about it in this group and will come to understand it and not be so afraid.

Then we talked about what are we really made of? Memories. That's what we are, everything is a memory. This makes sense, too. I need to ponder it more, though. Maybe I will read the book.

# August 19, 2013

Wow, been a week since I wrote in this. Thought about writing, but nothing came to me. Widowed Too Soon Group this evening really helped me. Tonight's topic and handout was Grief's Timing. Handout is by Dr. Earl A. Grollman.

This is what I learned:

Layers of grief are cognitive, physical, spiritual, and behavioral, as well as emotional.

> Emotionally – nerves are raw. They are short-tempered with all those around them. There is self-recrimination as they recall words of scorn and impatience, acts of exasperation and of churlishness "Nothing matters anymore, why go on?"

> Cognitively – It didn't happen. There must be some mistake. When the telephone rings, for a moment they think it is their loved one. There is difficulty in remembering events. "Is it Alzheimer's?" They talk out loud to the one who died. "Are they crazy?" Their chest becomes tight, the throat constricted and the stomach knotted.

> Physically – Aching hearts take a toll on the rest of the body with possible problems of sleep and

eating disorders, pounding headaches, dizziness, fatigue, back pain, strange rashes and other medical difficulties (even the symptoms that caused the death of their loved one).

<u>Spiritually</u> – Death is a journey into the unknown that may shake the mourner's faith. "Why me? Why am I being punished?" God may appear distant or vengeful. Eventually, in their struggle, they may gain greater spiritual insights to cope more effectively with their helplessness, guilt and loneliness.

Grief is not a disorder, a disease, or a weakness. It is an emotional, physical and spiritual necessity, the price they pay for love. Part of them has been buried with their beloved. The aftermath of the grieving process does not end when the body is buried and the flowers have withered.

So does time heal? Not necessarily. Time is neutral depending on what the bereaved do with their time. Are they using their time to relax physically, emotionally and spiritually? Are they using the time to seek friends and family for companionship, guidance, and support? Days by themselves do not bring relief and release.

Do not make the mistake of comparing one grief-stricken person with another. Mourning is lonely, intense and personal. No one goes through the exact same pilgrimage. No one on the planet has our fingerprints or DNA. We don't know their despair, they don't know ours.

Words like "closure" or "recovery" do not work. The definition of closure is the "act of ending" and recovery means "to bring back to a normal position." When a loved one dies, life is never the same or "settled." There are no hallelujah choruses indicating that we are back to normal and that path of sorrow is forever settled.

No timetable for grief. With death there is no accurate predictor of the length of time to grieve. Grief does not travel along a straight line and then disappear.

The timetable of grief is uncharted territory. The following life changes are the barometers of their progress. When they:

- No longer get choked up by looking at old pictures;
- Understand that there may be questions that have no satisfying answers;
- Forgive their loved one and themselves;
- Talk openly about their loved one by sharing stories of his or her life and legacy;
- Accept comfort and support even when it may be difficult;
- Enjoy the present by taking life day-by-day, hour-by-hour.

Time works best when old dreams are reshuffled with fresh plans by weaving the threads of the yesterdays with the tapestry of todays. As theologian Paul Tillich wrote, "In our present, our future and our past are ours."

That's what I learned from the handout. From the people at group, I learned it's OK to not accomplish something every day. It's OK to stay in bed sometimes. It's OK to still have Ron's things. I had to go through them since I had to move. Some people haven't touched anything. Who knows, if I was at our house, his Chiefs coat might still be hanging on the chair. His clothes might be in the dirty clothes basket. I probably would have things the way he left them. Tools still in the garage, his jalapenos still in the fridge, his ice cream still in the freezer. But, I had to move them and throw his food out. I had to let go of those things. I didn't want to, but I had to. I miss him so much. I learned I'm not the only one who doesn't eat at the table, who doesn't like to go eat out alone. Who feels supper time is the hardest sometimes. I learned it's OK that wherever I am in this grief process that it's OK. There's no reward to speed through it, but there is a price if I hurry. It's not a race. There isn't any place that says that almost at 2 years I'm supposed to be doing this or that, not this or not that. That all of our journeys are as different as our DNA. They may have some commonalities, but not the same. I knew that part. But the part that it's OK if I'm a bum some days. Grief is emotionally and physically draining. I do need structure.

Some days, structure and routine happen, other days--not even close. I think I'm ready to find a part-time job. I need a purpose. I need a reason to get up besides my animals. I need to be around people. I know that I need people. So, now maybe explore and get serious about finding a part-time job. Nothing physical cause of my fibro. Something that is rewarding. Something that I can enjoy, where I can do what God wants me to do, to use my pain to help others. I want to do that. But, I don't have a clue what that job is, where that job is, and when I will find it. I have been praying to God to show me what He wants me to do…how does He want to use me for His glory? I need clear signs – something to hit me on the head cause I'm pretty slow and clueless! It's so hard to be patient, though. Hard to wait for God's timing. I think I need a job now, I think I need money now, so I think He needs to show me what to do now. But, that's my thinking and my wanting it in my time–now. I don't know when He will show me, but I know He will. He will totally use me like He used Ron. Maybe not in the same way, but in His own way. I feel honored and humbled that somehow, some way, He will take this grief pain I'm full of and use it to help someone, somewhere, somehow.

Tonight was the 3rd week. We only have 3 left, then a six-week break. Not looking forward to a break.

# AUGUST 26, 2013

Group tonight was awesome. Our leader is in D.C. tonight, so a lady co-worker of his filled in for him. We went over Kuebler Ross' Stages of Grief. We had a great discussion.

When I arrived, I saw one of the ladies in our group had about 12 blue and white star balloons. She asked each of us to take a marker and write something on a balloon either to our spouse or to her husband. Today was the 2-year anniversary of her husband's death from cancer. I had seen people release balloons before, for different reasons, but I had never done it. I wrote a message to Ron on one side, to her husband on the other. I haven't talked much to the others in group, I noticed every time, though, how sad she looked. I could see and feel her pain. I wanted to reach out, but hadn't yet, but I felt that I would sometime, some way. This evening, she was smiling, even laughing some. I commented it was nice to see her smile. She sat by me in group and we talked some. While releasing the balloons and afterwards, we talked in the parking lot a little bit. We laughed and hugged. When I got in my car to leave, I thanked God for putting all those people in my life, but especially her. I'm not sure why. I can still see all those balloons floating in the sky, going north. One was just a tad bit away from the group. Not very far, just a tad. I figured that one was mine. I'm always the outcast, the rebel, the different one, the one on my own path, doing my own thing, going my own way.

Driving home, it popped in my head that on October 2nd, Ron's 2-year anniversary, our group will be on break. I don't like that idea very much. I also thought that maybe I should do a balloon release with his parents. Then I thought maybe invite our pastor and his friends from church and the tech team. Yeah, I like that idea a lot. Balloons need to be red and yellow stars. Those are Chiefs colors and Ron loved the Chiefs. They actually won a preseason game against the St. Louis Rams…in OVERTIME!!!!! Who woulda thunk it, the Chiefs actually won!!! Ron was a loyal, faithful, diehard fan–even though the Chiefs are so bad!!!

# OCTOBER 2, 2013

Balloon Release for Ron's Heaven Day

Today at 5:30 p.m., Ron's mom, dad, niece and family, people from Ron's and my small group, people from my new small group, people from tech arts, friends from church, and our awesome pastor gathered at church. I passed out red and gold balloons--Chiefs colors--and let people write a message to Ron and to someone in Heaven they miss.

Some people spoke about Ron and how he touched their life. How they remember him. I didn't talk and I didn't break down like I thought I would. Our pastor said a prayer and we all let our balloons go. It had been an overcast day, but at the time for releasing the balloons, the sun was out. It was beautiful watching all those balloons float away. Our church is very close to the interstate. I wonder what people driving thought when they saw 30-some balloons floating above them. Floating up towards Heaven.

It was peaceful. It was beautiful. My awesome father-in-law captured the whole event on camera. I can still see those balloons floating towards Heaven. Of all the 30-some people there, only two of them did not know Ron. Everyone else knew him before me. I was so grateful they took time out of their day to come to honor him. Many of us said we could see Ron shaking his head and grinning. I miss that so much.

Afterwards, my awesome in-laws took me out to eat. I love them so much. We talked about the balloon release and about Ron. It's just so weird without him with us. That empty spot at the table just breaks my heart. It has to be weird for them, too, having me there, but not Ron, their baby boy, there.

So now it's time to think about the holidays. I dread them. Ron loved them. Grief through the holidays is so hard. It's hard cause I know

Ron wouldn't want me to be sad. He would want me to enjoy them. I am luckier than the other widows/widowers in my group. They all had been married way longer than me and Ron. I can't imagine all the traditions they had together. All the memories they made together. It has to be horribly hard for them. I was without Ron for all but four years, so I was used to not being with him. But, I feel ripped off that I only got those four years. We didn't get that time to make our own traditions. To make all the memories, to do the things we wanted to do. They didn't happen. They won't ever happen. I'm not angry; I'm sad that I finally had Ron to share the holidays with and--BOOM–he's gone. It's not fair. I know God doesn't promise fair. But still...

My family ALWAYS, ALWAYS, ALWAYS waits till the last minute to plan Thanksgiving, Christmas, any other holiday or anything at all. I grew up that way. Didn't everyone do that?! No, people plan ahead. That's a foreign concept to me, though!

Ron's mom and dad asked me to go to Ron's brother and wife's in Indiana for Thanksgiving. I wanted to go, but panic set in. Ron and I went there with them in 2010. That was Ron's last Thanksgiving. I was so torn about going there. I love all of them and wanted to see them again. But, something always gave me a huge lump in my throat and knot in my stomach when I thought about going. Just like eating out, or doing anything with his family, that empty spot at the table, in the car all that way, him not being with us all visiting and hanging out. Just that thought broke my heart every time I thought about it. Every time. I thought I would be OK. I tried to convince myself I could do it. I also told myself to not be a wimp, to buck up and be strong. Those thoughts couldn't convince my heart that it would be OK. The days went by and it got closer and closer to Thanksgiving. Another reason I felt I should stay was for my kids and my sister. I didn't want to leave them alone with no place to go, no dinner, no family chaos. I was so torn, I talked to my grief counselor about how I wanted to go, but just didn't feel strong enough. Why couldn't I believe God would get me through it? He told me not to "put myself in a straight jacket." I needed a way out of the situation if I was having a hard time. Riding in the car from Kansas to Indiana is a long way with that empty spot in the back seat with me. There wouldn't be a way out. I couldn't, and wouldn't, jump out of the car along the way. If my emotions got the best of me, there was no escape. Same with being there without him. When visiting, laughing, eating, whatever it might be... if that moment hit me, I couldn't escape. Not if it hit me, but when it would. I know it would hit me. Maybe not every moment, but sometime, or many times, probably it would hit me that he wasn't there where he was with us for the last Thanksgiving on this Earth with us. Now he's gone. He's in Heaven and we are down here in this broken world, missing him. Missing his giggles. His silliness. His attitude, his smile, that silly grin, rolling his eyes, all those things we all love about him and miss. That void–too much for me. I could escape to a different room, but that wouldn't work for the whole trip. My counselor told me I needed to not overload my emotions on Thanksgiving, cause Christmas was coming. Great. Ron loved Christmas. It was his favorite holiday. Why do Thanksgiving and Christmas have to be so close together anyway? It's too hard. Not just for me, but for his family. For anyone who is going through any kind of grief. It's just too hard.

So, I decided not to go. I wasn't being a wimp like I told myself I was. I was taking care of myself and saving emotions for Christmas. I wanted to be there in Indiana in spirit, though. Or, I should say, I wanted to somehow honor Ron. To have him be there with his parents, his brother and family. I didn't want to leave him out. My grief counselor suggested making some kind of centerpiece to honor Ron. So, I asked Google, Pinterest, Etsy, and searched for hours and hours for something easy to make, cheap and fast. Those are my requirements for almost everything I do. Easy, cheap and fast. I saw something called a Thanksgiving Tree. I changed it up a bit to make it meet what I wanted. I decided to make two--one to go to Indiana and one to be at our little Thanksgiving here. I found two branches, bought terra cotta pots, river rocks, and made leaves from orange, red, yellow and brown construction paper. I found some leaves outside to use as patterns. Oh, yeah, did you know that for some insane reason there is no brown construction paper in the pack I bought? Really? No brown? That was messed up, but Ron's dad came to the rescue, as always, and had some brown. So, I traced, I cut, I poked pinholes in each leaf, I cut thread to hang each leaf with. I went a little nuts cutting so many leaves. I think I have leaves for a few more Thanksgivings! As my counselor suggested, I wrote out my leaves. I wrote about Ron on some, my mom and dad, my granddaughters, about God, and sent it off to Indiana with them. I did the same here with my sister, son and daughter. It wasn't such a great hit like I hoped it would be here. My point was more of things to be thankful for. I was hoping to get them to realize that even though life may not be the way we want it to be here, we are still very blessed. I was laughed at and made fun of for my little tree at our dinner. It's OK. I tried. I can't make others be thankful or feel blessed. Maybe next year. I kept the branch, and the pot, and the rocks, and the leaves. I will try again. I'm kinda curious what my leaves will say next year. I kept the ones on there this year. Others did put some leaves on, finally. I don't know if it was to humor me, or if it was genuine, or to get me to stop asking and begging. It was a strange thing to have a branch in a pot with rocks and paper leaves. It's different and that's just who I am. I will say that writing those thoughts on those leaves for the one that went to Indiana and the one here, it helped. Writing helps me. Paper doesn't judge you. It doesn't mock you, it's just paper. But, it gets those thoughts out, and something about writing what's in your head is just very therapeutic for me.

# CHRISTMAS 2013

It was a rough time. My life was crazy with family stuff happening. Stuff I'm not gonna say in this book, but stuff that has been very stressful, painful, and never-ending. But, good things happened, too. I did fun things with friends. I drove two hours to get a six-week-old Lab puppy I named Willow. I could see Ron shaking his head like I'm crazy. I am crazy. Hi, my name is Susan and I am crazy. I would drive to the ends of the earth for a dog. My Lab, Sophie, died in my/Ron's chair September 3rd of this year. I missed her horribly. There's just something about a Lab. I wanted a female Chocolate Lab. I wanted a puppy so I didn't have to deal with getting a dog with cat issues, like Jake who was a bull in a china shop. Or who had separation anxiety like Sophie had. I knew a puppy was going to be a ton of work. But I needed a distraction. I needed a Lab. Okay, I wanted a Lab. In my world, I needed it! I checked the local shelter. I checked shelters around here. I checked rescues. I firmly believe in rescuing, adopting, not buying from a breeder or a pet store. I believe in saving a life. I spent one whole Monday searching on Craigslist. I searched my town. I searched about six other towns in this state. Then I searched Nebraska. I found some that were Lab/Blue Heeler mix in Lincoln, Nebraska. I never had a Blue Heeler. I liked the looks of them. I read about the breed and decided that for where I live, it wasn't a good fit. I found some in Kansas City. I wanted a female Chocolate Lab. These Chocolate Labs were male, the black ones were female. I prayed about it overnight. Labs go fast, especially at Christmas time. The next morning, I was walking Lucky and talking to God. That's always my "God time." I thank Him, ask Him stuff, I pray to Him, I just have my morning conversations with Him. I asked Him what to do. I wanted a female Chocolate Lab. Should I settle for chocolate male? For a black female? When I got back home, I searched the places again. Bingo!!!! Female Chocolate Lab 2 hours away!! Of course, I called and asked some questions and asked to have one held till the next day when I could get there. Well, there were questions I didn't think to ask and things I should have done differently. I always learn the hard way!

I got her that next morning. When I saw her, I knew I had to get her. Not just because she was an adorable baby Chocolate female Lab, but because she looked malnourished. She had worms, bad. She had urine and feces on her. After talking to people days afterwards, I believe she was a puppy-mill puppy. So, I rescued her. She's turned my house upside down and I am sleep-deprived from a baby puppy not sleeping through the night yet. But, she has kept me very busy with these few weeks before Christmas.

Christmas was hard. It was hard in lots of ways. I still miss my mom and dad. I miss Ron. I miss lots of people I no longer see for lots of reasons. But, I am very thankful and am very blessed for the people God did put in my life now. I am thankful for all my friends and family. Christmas was weird this year. There were last-minute changes in plans, but I'm used to that! I didn't get to Christmas Eve Service this year, but my daughter and I spent Christmas Eve with Ron's mom and dad and nieces and their families. I loved being there. I love all of them. It was hard being there without Ron. It just doesn't feel right without him there. He loved Christmas. He loved his family. He loved to eat! But, most of all, he loved Jesus and the whole reason for the season. He wasn't about materialistic stuff. He was about celebrating the meaning of Christmas. He was celebrating in Heaven. Remember the poem I shared earlier? Yeah, it still makes me cry. And, I'm jealous cause I can't wait to spend Christmas in Heaven.

Christmas Day was good. My kids were here. We did something totally weird. We watched movies together. I honestly do not remember the last time I spent Christmas with just my two kids, and not other family members. It was good. Weird, but good.

Well, Christmas and all the chaos and everything was finally over. I could take a deep breath and relax. Willow kept me super busy, like a newborn--always had to be supervised so she didn't chew on something she shouldn't or didn't have an accident. Potty training in winter wasn't a bright idea. Willow doesn't sleep through the night, so taking her outside at all hours of the night gets a little bit cold, but she's totally worth it!

Just when I think that it's down time, I realized Ron's 48th birthday was almost here. I forgot about it. How could I forget his birthday? Great. What do I do? I need to honor him, do something special for people to make him proud. I needed to be able to see him shake his head, grin and roll his eyes at me! So, since I always have to do things the hard way and do things at the last minute, I finally had the idea for Ron's birthday. I took the picture the Tech Arts Director took of Ron and the L-3 journal Ron wrote his last journal entry in to the print shop. I love supporting locally-owned businesses. This is where I have my Watkins and Herbalife business cards printed. The owner is very awesome and does excellent work. Oh, yeah, she also does her magic fast cause I am always giving her projects at the last minute! I asked her if she could make my idea a reality. I knew what I wanted, but didn't have a clue how to do it myself. She worked her magic and put Ron's picture and his journal entry into one big picture. I had copies made for Ron's parents, some other family members, and some staff at church. It was amazing. Ron's last photo and Ron's last Bible journal entry. His last prayer before he collapsed in my arms and made that last sound I never want to hear again.

# January 9, 2014

Ron's birthday. Ron isn't here to celebrate it. Ron is spending his birthday in Heaven. I'm sure it's the best birthday party ever. I had an appointment with my grief counselor in the morning. I took the picture I had made and told him about what I planned to do with it. I really get mad at myself for not thinking things through sometimes! I needed something to put with the picture to say what the picture and journal entry meant and why I was giving it to people. I am very technologically challenged. I don't have a computer to type something up on or to print it out. I didn't even have a clue what I wanted to say. Nothing like waiting till the last minute! I went to a friend's shop cause I knew she would be able to make something up for me fast and make it all OK. I also didn't think about how to present these pictures to staff at church so they wouldn't get bent, and I needed a way to put names on them. They were too big for the mailboxes. My friend gave me flat rate boxes to put the pics in between and wrap. I wanted to use Happy Birthday paper. I did know that much! I decided I would go buy mailing bubble envelopes. Time was running out, I needed to have these at church by 5 p.m. My friend had what I asked her to print up, all printed on happy yellow cardstock, a border around it, and cut in just the right size--all before I got envelopes bought and four of the pictures wrapped!

I went and picked them up. Zoomed home and wrapped each picture to give to staff at church and his parents. I taped the yellow printed card on front. Went to put the card on front. Went to put the picture in the envelope. Guess what? By wrapping the picture, it just barely was too big for the envelope. All the time stressing about how to protect the picture was for nothing. Oh well, Wal-Mart will give me my money back for all of them. Time was ticking away. I was only going to be able to just wrap them in the Happy Birthday paper and pass them out that way. I didn't do a very good job of wrapping them because I was running out of time. I was afraid I was going to have to take them there tomorrow. That would make me very sad because today was Ron's birthday. Not tomorrow. And the cards my awesome friend printed said today, January 9, 2024, on them. Tomorrow won't work. I prayed and prayed and wrapped and wrapped. I walked in the door at 4:40. I know cause I looked at the clock!! Finally!!! Done and ready to give them to staff. I love my church. I felt this amazing peace as soon as I walked in the door. I told the secretary it's Ron's birthday. I handed her her package. I watched her read the card taped on front. I watched her smile. I watched her unwrap it and smile again. The tech arts director and worship leader were there. I told them it was Ron's birthday. I handed them their package. The secretary told me our lead pastor was not in. One pastor was meeting with someone. Some of the others were busy. I asked if the pastor who was with us all that horrible day and who did Ron's service was there. He and another pastor were there. I told him it was Ron's birthday. I handed them their packages. The associate pastor had a copy of Ron's last journal by his computer where he sees it every day. I am so very blessed to have all these people in my life. Ron loved this church. Ron loved them and I am so thankful Ron made himself available to God to be used to lead me here. I still don't like Topeka, but I don't plan on leaving anytime soon…unless God leads me somewhere to be used for something I don't have a clue about.

Oh, yeah, I'm sure Ron was watching me run around like a crazy woman today, trying to get this done. Yep, I can see him shake his head, roll his eyes and grin. I really miss that.

I gotta back up a little bit. Remember my author friend? Well, she read what I had written so far, gave this notebook back to me and moved to the East Coast the next day! I remember when she handed me this notebook back and told me to keep writing, I asked her "What's the next step?" She said it needs to be proofed. Proofed? Hmmmm...you can tell I never wrote a book before! I asked how that happens. How do I find someone to do that? OK, here's where God did something amazing again! She told me the name of the person she had proof her book. Really? You're kidding? She is a friend from church! Her husband served on the tech team with Ron. Since his death, she has been extremely supportive. But, I had no clue she was a proofer! So, again, I always do things the hard way and at the last minute. My friend had been sick most of the summer, and life was crazy for both of us. I didn't want to ask her to proof this until I could meet with her in person and have her read what I have written so far. So, December 31st we met at Subway for lunch. Chatted a little bit, I told her what my friend said about proofing. She is a speed reader, which is good cause that afternoon she and her husband were moving to Iowa! Now, I really believe God has a sense of humor. I mean, really? Put me in an anger group when I don't have an anger problem, but meet a person who is an author who accidently happens to become an awesome friend, who encourages me to keep writing this, then God moves her to the East Coast!?!? Then–it so happens that her proofer is a friend of mine who reads this, then He moves her to Iowa the day she reads this. What's up with this anyway? BUT...God is so amazing and here is why. He is always up to something. When my friend and I were wrapping up our time together, she said she could proof this from Iowa, then she told me about someone else at church who has written three books. One was made into a documentary. I didn't recognize this person's name, but she gave me her number. OK, remember I told you I'm a wimp? I guess the fear settled in now. I knew I wouldn't feel comfortable calling someone out of the blue and asking to read this and proof it. Well, the really cool thing is that God knew this, too. He just constantly blows my mind because a week after I said goodbye to my friend and she moved to Iowa, my in-laws and my sister and I were eating supper at church. This couple sat down with us. My in-laws and I never met these two. Everyone talked chit-chat–no big deal. I remember I got up to go to the little girls' room, came back and sat down. It was getting late and staff was starting to clean up the kitchen and close down. My sister and in-laws left the table to get ready to leave. Then, the most amazing conversation happened. While I was gone, Ron's dad told them about Ron passing. After they all left the table, this very kind lady asked if I knew her son-in-law. He served on the tech team and attended Ron's funeral. When she said his name, it was a good thing I was already sitting down because her son-in-law was married to the person my friend told me about who wrote three books! I had been sitting with this person's parents and had no clue! I told her my story of writing this and about my friend who read it and encouraged me to keep writing, told me about my friend who proofed it and she moved to the East Coast. I told her about that friend who read this and gave me her daughter's name and moved to Iowa! I told her I was a wimp and was afraid to call her daughter. God knew that! So, being the amazing God that He is, He put her parents at our table that night at church? Who woulda thunk it? You can't make this stuff up! I left church, just shaking my head. I still shake my head in awe. It's a God thing…totally a God thing. He used my friends, too. He uses people to do things they have no clue about. Wow, just wow! I gave her my number. I can't wait for this part of the journey, to meet the next people God is giving me to make this book happen. And the cool part is that so far, they have all been Christians and go to my awesome church! Again, who woulda thunk it? God did! One thing I am kinda confused on is how am I going to know when this book is done? My story is how God used Ron to lead me here and put awesome people in my life and prepared me for when Ron was gone. Ron has been gone for 27 months now. But, grief is ongoing. God's work and provision for me is ongoing. It isn't going to end, so how am I going to know when to end this book? I asked a couple of people this past week. Both of them told me that God will let me know when it's time. So, I will trust them and trust God for His direction cause I know I can't figure it out on my own!

Grief is very much ongoing. Some days, I'm fine; some days, I'm not fine. It's like a winding path that sometimes takes me back to where I started. Sometimes, I get quite a way on this path, then a sharp turn takes me back, or off in a totally different direction.

The "Through a Season of Grief", which is a devotional book

by Bill Dunn and Kathy Leonard, really helps me. Or I read "From Mourning to Joy"...whichever one fits my mood that day. My moods don't go in order; everyone's grief is different. No one grieves the same way or at the same time. So, on Ron's birthday, I looked up how I felt that day. I was amazed that the page that I felt fit was page 248. The last page I read was page 56, "Healthy Grieving: Step Four". Wow, that page was awesome! The first two sentences say "The fourth step in healthy grieving is to tell your story to others. Give someone an honest account of your loss." It's about talking to people about your grief. I don't have a problem doing that. I have family, Ron's mom and dad, my church family, friends, and this writing. I talk all the time. Honestly, writing helps the most, besides my Widowed Too Soon group and individual grief counseling. Those have been a huge blessing. I missed most of the group in November and December, but hopefully in February when it starts back up, I can get there more. I love the prayer at the bottom of page 56. It says "Lord Jesus, You know what is best for me, much more than I ever will. Open my heart and my mouth and enable me to share my story with others. Amen." Wow! It's just like that was written just for me!

Ron's birthday was healing...something about having his picture and journal entry put together as one picture, passing them out to some of the staff at church and Ron's mom and dad. It was pretty stressful getting it all done, but the actual giving of them was kinda peaceful, a release, even a kind of joy, in a weird way. So, after the craziness of that day, I sat down with the grief book. Page 248 fit. The title is "Letting Go". The first paragraph says "To move on means (1) you have to acknowledge that things will never be the same again and (2) you have to desire God's plan for your life now. Letting go of a lost one is tough, especially when the love is deep, and he or she has filled a need in you that was never filled until you met this person". BINGO!!!

Again, it was like these words were written just to me. I was a single parent, working two jobs I loved for eight years. One of those jobs was on the night shift. I was so sleep-deprived. I felt horrible that I couldn't spend the time I wanted and needed with my kids and family. Being a single parent is rough. Before those jobs, I went to K-State. When I started, my daughter was in first grade. My son was a year old. I lived off financial aid. My parents didn't pay my way through school. It was a dream of mine to go to college. Well, honestly, my dream was to go to college in Colorado with my high school friends from Colby. That didn't happen. We all went different ways, life happened, and here I was, a single parent, finally going to college. I loved K-State, but didn't get to do the whole college life thing. I had two kids. I got up every morning, took my daughter to school, my son to daycare or family, and went to classes. I did arrange my classes so I could go to the Union and watch "The Young and The Restless"! That was stupid! I also scheduled in study time when I could. Once I got home with the kids, it was "mom mode". It was help with homework, laundry, supper, baths, and bedtime. It was usually between 10:00 p.m. and midnight before I got to start on homework. I would study until 3:00, 4:00, or 5:00 a.m., go to bed and get up at 7:00 a.m., and do it all over again. I'm not complaining. I'm very thankful I had family to watch them when I needed help, especially during tests, finals, papers, etc. I was very blessed. I did get upset when people who did not know me or my situation would ask why I didn't get a job. When on Earth was I supposed to work? I never slept anyway! Then, I had my two jobs for eight years. I loved them. Both were in mental health. Yeah, I know what you are thinking, and yes, I blended in with the clients very well! The clients at both jobs were a very special part of my life. I loved working with the severely and persistently mentally ill. I saw people go from living in institutions to living in the community, with our help. I also saw them at their lowest, off their meds, depressed, or suicidal. Sadly, one favorite client did commit suicide. That broke my heart. My clients were a huge part of my life. I actually saw them more than my family. Many days, I worked from 8:00 a.m. to 10:00 p.m.--then on weekends, from 8:00 a.m. to 10:00 p.m.--then worked at the mental health unit from 11:00 a.m. to 7:00 p.m. I ran my body down. I was always taking care of everyone else but me. It was my "normal" to go 36 to 48 hours with very little sleep, several times a week, especially on weekends. Then, fibromyalgia set in. It rocked my world. It was so bad that I could hardly lift a gallon of milk. If clients needed to go to the grocery store or Wal-Mart, I usually had to ride in the motorized cart. The pain was awful. I missed work. Many days, I could not walk without holding onto something. I remember days closing my office door and crying my eyes out because my pain was so bad. Many times, I did that in the morning after I got there. But, I loved my job and my clients. They needed me. I thought staff turnover was high. People got burned out, went to grad school, or went to better jobs. I was always there. Clients knew I was there for them. They knew I wasn't going to leave them. They were like my other family. But, eventually, only a few months after fibromyalgia attacked my body, I had to quit my day/evening job. It was too hard on my body. The agency was going through downsizing and I was gonna be let go anyway. It was just a matter of time. I just worked my night shift job at the mental health unit. I still saw my clients, but not all the time. I missed them a lot. But, now when I saw them, it was only when they were in crisis.

Now, back to the part about "a need not being met until you met that person". I didn't go to church all those years. Actually, I did go to one in Manhattan a few times, but work got in the way a lot. It was OK, but I never really felt welcomed or felt like I fit in. I was pretty shy and not very good at starting conversations. I believed in God. I always believed in God. I just didn't have a clue that there was more to it. I never heard of a personal relationship with Jesus. I talked to God. I prayed to God. I even begged God. But, I didn't understand that He wasn't there to do what I asked or prayed or begged for. I didn't understand why He wasn't answering my prayers. "If only" He would do this, or "if only" God would do that, life would be OK. My mom always reminded me of God's timing, God's purpose, and God's plan. It didn't make sense. I thought I had to earn my way to Heaven and if He wasn't helping me get what I thought I needed, then how was I going to get there? So, that need wasn't there. Not until Ron entered my life. It still blows my mind that all those years of wondering why God never gave me a husband, why He wanted me to struggle instead of being like more of my co-workers who were married and didn't have to do everything alone. I didn't have to do everything alone. I had family and they helped me all the time, probably too much. My parents would give me or my siblings their very last penny if we needed it. They shouldn't have, but they did. They believed if they had anything--it didn't matter what--that if someone needed it, they gave it to them or us. So, when in March of 2007 I met Ron, I knew he was different. He treated me like I have never been treated before. He spoiled me. I was ecstatic to not have to pump gas. Guess what? Now, I have to put gas in the vehicle again. But, Ron making himself available for God to use, changed my life. Then, God really changed my life by taking Ron to be with Him instead of being with me. Little did I know that "Till death do us part" meant only four years. Those four years were not perfect. It wasn't a fairy tale with my prince on a white horse, but it was a much better life because now God was the major focus. My friends were real and didn't make fun of me because I was a newbie to the Bible. I still don't understand all of it. I am not as dedicated to my Bible journal as Ron was. I'm a work in progress, though. I can always start again, catch up, and be in awe of how much better life is if I remember to do what Ron did…give God his first and his best, not his last and his leftovers. I still can hear our pastor saying that. So, the need that was filled was the need for Jesus. The need to know I can't earn my way to Heaven. I can't ever be good enough because God only compares us to Jesus, not to each other. So, we all fall way short. None of us are as good as Jesus. Sorry if I burst someone's bubble, but we just aren't that good.

The next paragraph on that page says "to really admit to yourself", 'this person is gone and life's got to go on, and I've got to buck up and turn the corner and get going' is probably one of the toughest transitions in the grief process", says Dr. Joseph Stowell. Then it goes on, "Your plan for life was suddenly changed". Got that right! But, God has a purpose for you, and you were created to fulfill that purpose. That is why you are here on Earth right now. Find God's plan for your life and seek fulfillment from Him! "The Lord will fulfill His purpose for men, your love, Oh Lord, endures forever; do not abandon the works of your hands" (Psalm 138:8). "But I have raised you up for this purpose, that I might show you my power and that my name might be proclaimed in all the Earth" (Exodus 9:16). This page ends with this prayer: "Lord God, things will never be the same again, and I will never be able to go back to the way things were. I admit this, Lord, and I will move forward with a purpose, seeking to fulfill your plan for my life. What do you have for me to do? Amen." Wow! Those are powerful words for me right now!

# JANUARY 13, 2014

Tonight, as I look up at the clear night sky and the full moon and all the bright, shiny stars, I'm reminded of a card I got from a co-worker when my mother passed away four years ago. It was a card with a picture of a moon and stars. On the inside, it said something like "stars are peepholes in heaven for our loved ones to look down and see us". I love that idea. A few years ago, I read a book that said our loved ones cannot look down and see us because that might make them sad and there is no sadness in Heaven. I don't like that thought. I've always been told that such and such is looking down on me. That is a very comforting thought. I guess I'm just choosing to believe that Ron, my parents, my grandparents, aunt, uncles, brother-in-law, and others I know have beat me to Heaven can all peek through those holes we call stars. At night, in bed, if the sky is clear, I can see a few stars outside my window. One star caught my attention one night. Maybe it looked bigger or brighter, I don't remember. I look at that star every night that it is visible. Call me crazy, cause I am, but I also talk to that star. After I pray, I say "hi" to Ron, "hi" to mom and dad, "hi" to grandma and grandpa, "hi" to my brother-in-law. Except for Ron two years ago and my mother four years ago, an aunt and an uncle, most have been gone many years. I still miss them, though. Each person had an important role in my life and now there is a void. No one can take their place. Anyway, I talk to them. I tell them all that I miss them. I tell them about my day. I tell them what's happening and I tell them all that I love them. It may sound crazy, but that's who I am. I love the sky, the clouds, the blue sky, the rain; and I totally love seeing huge, fluffy snowflakes falling from the sky! I adore and cherish sunsets. I'm still waiting for my ship to come in so I can have that cabin with a deck to the west to see the sunset and a porch to the east, just in case I'm ever up in time to see a sunrise! I am always amazed and in awe at each sunset I see. I can't see them where I live now. Maybe a tiny bit, but I want a view of the sky, the whole sky, so I can plan my day around sitting in a rocking chair, watching the sunset. I never get tired of seeing them. Some people don't get too excited and don't care. To many people, sunsets just happen... so what? To me, each one is amazing, beautiful, ever-changing, and it's like God is trying to get our attention to stop and watch and notice what He is doing. How He is painting the sky like a masterpiece. It just does something to my soul.

On November 8, of this past year, I drove to Norton, KS for a vendor event a friend was putting on. I met her a month before at a show in Colby that a long-lost friend put on. That whole thing is another story, but totally a God thing! Anyway, until I drove to Colby in October, this trip to Norton was only the second time I drove that far by myself. I was kinda nervous, but I knew God was with me every minute, so it would be OK. About ten miles out of town, I lost cell service. It reminded me that back in the olden days, people traveled all the time without cell phones. I was lost without any service, but had my radio set on the only station I listen to, K-LOVE. I didn't get that station very long either. I know Kansas is made fun of a lot, but seriously? No cell service and no K-LOVE? I did have a whopping two CDs, though. I'm not big on CDs. I think Ron had about 150-200 of them. Mine are Casting Crowns and Big Daddy Weave. I listened to those over and over the whole drive there, which was about 4 ½ hours or so. It was just me in the car, so I did not harm anyone by my singing!

My goal was to be in Norton before dark. I might have made it except that I kinda missed the sign saying when to turn left and go west. I realized I missed it when I saw the "Welcome to Nebraska" sign! Geeze, if there is any way I can get lost, I will make it happen! It was a quick fix, though, since I was only a few miles north...no biggie. The trip there was pretty uneventful except for when the sun started to set. It was the time of year when deer like to jump in front of vehicles and make people crash. I can still see that sky changing colors. But, it was more than changing colors! It was like God knew I was tired, but needed coaxing not to worry about the sun going down. I think that was the most amazing sunset I have ever seen. It was like God was saying "It's OK, come on, keep driving this way, it's OK!" God kept changing those oranges, pinks and purples, and I could honestly feel a tug to keep going and not freaking out cause it was getting dark. I wasn't very late; it was just very dark—it was October in Kansas! I followed that tug. When I did get to Norton, I was very relieved, but I also was so thankful that God coaxed me with the sunset, saying "it's OK, keep looking, keep driving". It kept me awake. Listening to my Christian CDs and watching the sunset in the huge, open sky again—a picture I don't think I will ever get out of my head. God took care of getting me there safely. He painted the sky in colors only He can do. I didn't need the cell because I had God, and God had my back!

# February 13, 2014

Besides the beauty of the sunsets God gives us, I love snow. Snow, to me, is absolutely beautiful. I am most happy and feel most at peace, when it's snowing and I'm snowed in. I especially love the huge, fluffy flakes and watching them dance to their landing on trees, roofs, cars, the ground, or whatever is beneath them. To me, snow makes them beautiful. It's just so peaceful and relaxing and quiet. Thunderstorms are loud and not peaceful to me. I love the beauty of the storm clouds and lightning, but that's it. I love rain, just not storms. Ron hated snow, and he hated the cold; if it was 75 degrees or colder, he was cold. Anything over 75 degrees was hot to me. One winter, we had a lot of snow at Christmas. Ron, being the "doer" and "get it done" person, spent hours shoveling out our driveway, sidewalk, and his pickup in the street. One of my very favorite pictures I have of him is that day when he peeked through the glass door, shovel in hand, with his long hair and in his Chiefs coat.

He was pooped from shoveling, but was smiling about how crazy he thought I was for liking this stuff. So, my dream of living in Colorado or someplace in the mountains wasn't his dream! He wanted warm—all year warm. Not me! So, whenever it snows, I remember how he felt about snow and that day he dug us out.

A week ago, we got 13 inches of snow. I woke up and there was just a dusting and I was so upset. I thought the snow went around us and I was not gonna be happy! So, of course, I posted my unhappiness on Facebook, and I was reassured the snow just wasn't here yet. OK. It was going to be OK; I just get impatient waiting on snow. So, I was happily snowed in for two days. I also think of how God put me where I live now because I do not have to shovel anything. The parking lot is cleared and the sidewalks cleaned and salted, right up to my front door. I think of Ron and how he would have loved to not have to shovel! On the third day, I ventured out into the world. The kid in me is a very happy camper, getting to tromp through snow. I will go out of my way to find snow to tromp in. I refuse to grow up. I went into the grocery store and boom!!! I slipped on some water from others' shoes. I landed on my right shoulder and arm. Some nice guy behind me helped me up. A lady from the floral department, I think, came and asked me if I was OK. I was just embarrassed and sore. With fibromyalgia, anything like that triggers a nice, long fibro flare-up. I should have reported it, but I didn't. I just wanted to get my stuff and get out of there. I was in pain for several days. I didn't want a doctor bill and pain pills never really help me anyway, so I didn't go. That happened on a Thursday. That Sunday, I was taking my dogs out the first thing in the morning and my Westie must have spotted a squirrel or something. She pulled me down while I was trying to shut the sliding door so Ron's cat wouldn't go outside. That "pull" yanked my back. The arm that I fell on earlier was in the door, so that day was very painful. I hobbled around, holding onto doorknobs, furniture, walls, or anything to help me walk. The next day or two was also painful, but not as bad as Sunday. I am very thankful that I did not hit my head either time I fell. Fibro flare-ups last several days. On Wednesday, I was just being a bum all day, napping on the loveseat with my puppies. A thought popped into my head and wouldn't leave. I was wishing Ron was here cause he always took care of me when I was in pain. Wait, he always took care of me, just more, when I was in pain. He loved to cook and clean and I was very happy to let him. Looking around my place now, my floors need vacuumed, trash needed taken out, and somebody needed to make me supper! Oh, yeah, and the dogs need taken out. Willow loves the snow and is constantly at the door wanting out just so she can go stick her whole face in the snow! She has a method to her madness because she knows to go to the door to tell me she needs to go potty. So, if I tell her "no" when she goes to the door for the zillionth time after she already went potty, then I think she will think she shouldn't go to the door. No, I absolutely do think she knows that I don't want to tell her "no" for going to the door. So, at 3 ½ months, she is outsmarting me...I'm in trouble!

Back to Ron. I was being selfish, wanting him here to cook and clean and take care of me and take the dogs out. I always want him here, just more so when I really need his help. So, I was thinking...what is Ron doing in Heaven? I know he's worshipping God, walking with Jesus, and in a place I am so curious about. One book I read awhile back said we will have jobs in Heaven. Hmmm... what's Ron's job? And when we are told there is a room being prepared for us, what does Ron's room look like? This book also said we recognize each other, but there is no marriage in Heaven. So, my tiny brain is trying to imagine seeing Ron again, knowing and loving Ron, but not living together? That's weird, in my little brain. And if we will have new, perfect bodies, how can that be if we don't have our physical bodies in Heaven? If our souls are in Heaven, what do our souls look like? How will Ron look the same, except with a new body, if he doesn't have a body? These may be crazy things to think, but I don't know why it's bugging me. So, for some reason, this evening while putting away some clothes in my dresser, I decided to look in Ron's wallet. I keep it in my drawer, but I don't know why. I see it all the time and just smile. It's probably been about a year since I opened it. Still no money! Not much there... just a few pictures, a few business cards, a couple of cards from our church (I'm guessing for him to pass out to people), cards for his truck and medical insurance—that's it! I had to laugh at myself. If I died tonight and people went through my purse, it would take them awhile! Probably no money, either, but lots of other stuff. Lots of business cards from Watkins, my handmade stuff called With Love, and cards from my vendor friends. Plus, my very important Dillons discount card, debit card, library card, and other stuff I keep for absolutely no good reason. That just shows our personality differences again. Ron was very simple and very practical. He didn't keep stuff he didn't need. He was not a stuff person! I just can't wrap my brain around how people don't need, want, or keep stuff. My mother taught me to be a very good stuff person. She kept everything. I am better than I used to be. Ron tried his hardest to teach me about stuff. Stuff isn't eternal--it's just stuff. My stuff is hard to get rid of. Everything has a story. When we were packing to move from Manhattan to here, the poor guy would pick up something and ask if I wanted to pack it or donate it or trash it. Well, I also have a huge problem answering a "yes" or "no" problem! I always had to tell him the story about whatever it was he was asking about. Being the practical person, he would ask that question I hated—was I going to USE it? What did it matter if I never did and probably wouldn't ever use it? If it had a story, it had a purpose, a reason for having it. Most of my stuff was from garage sales, but that didn't give it any less meaning. Some of my most prized possessions are from garage sales or thrift shops. So, after patiently listening to my stories about a zillion things, he would usually shake his head like "OK, but I don't understand why you want to keep it!" Some things were silly things from restaurants, such as their cool coasters or just a napkin that I kept because I really liked the place. We had the biggest U-Haul they made, I think. And it was stuffed!! But, also, there was the stuff in the car and in his pickup, which took several trips. When everything was out of there, I looked around and thought how much bigger it looked without all that stuff. I did throw away a lot of stuff, too. I donated a lot, but not as much as I should have. After Ron passed away and I had to move here, I donated way more stuff. But, I still kept more than I should have. I had to downsize a lot because this place is smaller. But, there is a basement that we didn't have before. When I go down to do laundry or something, I look around and ask myself "why did I bring all this stuff?" I have learned a lot more about stuff and how to not worship my stuff or other people's stuff. There are still some things I want. I have always wanted a purple VW Bug. A hippie VW bus for camping and a cabin with a deck to the west, to sit and watch the sunsets. Oh, yeah, and a log bed and log furniture for our house. And some land with the cabin for my dogs, of course. And the adorable alpacas. I think I have narrowed it down to just that stuff. I need a place to live, right? Why not a cabin? I need furniture and a bed, right? So, why not log? The sunsets are very therapeutic to me. I am always in awe of them. They take my breath away. Why not have a place to sit and watch them? To have my God time? It makes perfect sense to me. And the Bug? Well, just because I am a kid and they are a blast to drive. I only had one, a 1968 VW Bug. It did great on gas because it rarely ran! I had it towed so many times! My kids were young, but they remember being stranded in that thing. But, it got in my blood. I'm getting old, but someday I will have my K-State purple Bug! And the bus? Well, it makes perfect sense to me to have it because if I want to go places, why not have my bus (flower power, peace signs, smiley faces) to sleep in? It would be cheaper than a motel. Motels are boring and I could get bed bugs, or fungus from nasty carpet. You wouldn't want me to do that, right? But, the coolest part is that my animals could come along, too! It gets expensive boarding three animals. I miss them horribly and it stresses them out. How can they possibly be comfortable in a cage for days? That's just not right. Motels or B&Bs don't always think my animals are as awesome as I do. But, they do like to charge extra for them. But, the best reason for having a bus is because campsites and RV parks are off the beaten path. I love nature and being close to nature is important to me. It brings me peace, it calms me, and it refreshes my spirit. Being outside with fresh air is relaxing and is my God time. Just like the sunsets, nature is God's masterpiece. Trees, sky, stars, moon, flowers, water, animals, mountains, valleys…how can you not want to just sit or hike and explore and thank God for all of His creation? I don't like snakes, spiders, or flies. But, as long as they don't bother me, they are OK. Oh, yeah, ants are annoying, too. And wasps. I know God made each one for a reason. I just don't want to be up close and personal with them.

Back to Ron. I put his wallet back in my drawer and looked at his picture on top of my dresser. His grin made me smile. It's like he was saying "see, not much stuff in my wallet, huh?" Since Ron wasn't a stuff person, he didn't leave much stuff. I donated a lot of his clothes. I kept a box of my favorite clothes, or his favorites…just one box. I gave his parents some things—things that had connections to them or him when he was younger. I kept his CDs and his few movies and all of his Rolling Stone magazines. I have these all in my tiny living room and see them constantly. I never used any of these, so I don't need them. I don't ever listen to his CDs. I don't know why; I just don't. Ron loved music. I love music and am sure I would find ones I liked. It's almost like they are off-limits, like I don't think it's right to mess with them. He was meticulous. They had a certain order. It's not that they would ever get out of order if I used them. It just seems wrong to touch them. Is it because they are Ron's and are an idol? Or because they are Ron's and I'd probably lose it listening to them cause he loved them? I remember he told me his CDs were the only thing he and his first wife fought over when they divorced. Told ya that music was very important to him. I'm not a movie person. I almost always fall asleep watching it. He has several movies and we watched a few together. And then there is the Dale, Jr. one I bought him once. He was busy and never got to watch it. It's never been opened and is a collector's item. And all of his Rolling Stone magazines…I never look at them. I need to find some protectors for them, probably. And he had some Bibles and Christian books. That's Ron's stuff. That's most of what he had, besides his tools and things he had in our garage. Our house was the first house he lived in after leaving home. So, this was his first garage to have yard care things, tools, and all that manly stuff. In the back, was an old built-in workshop space. He kept that immaculate, too. So, he had his space— and then the rest was my stuff. When I went through the garage, sorting and tossing to move, I felt horrible. All that stuff (and my son had stuff there, too)—all that stuff that cluttered it up. He hated it, but never threw it away. He gently asked and hinted. But, again, everything had a story…so much guilt just over keeping stuff that now I wish I would not have kept. Guilt that he hated it, but lovingly tolerated it… all that stuff. This May is the yearly garage sale in my complex. I have now decided I will go through my stuff and attempt to sell it. What doesn't sell, I will donate. It's just stuff. If I'm not using it, it needs to bless someone else. Because we are never promised tomorrow, I need to get rid of stuff so that when I am gone, my kids, grandkids, and family don't have to spend precious time going through my stuff. I need to make it as easy as Ron made it for me. Besides, I probably don't have much that any of them will actually want. I might as well sell or donate it so they don't have to mess with it. It's just stuff. What really matters is God, His Word, and people. SEE, I really DO pay attention when I go to church. Stuff is not eternal.

# March 10, 2014

While doing Bible study this evening, I accidentally caught a glimpse of the sky looking like it was on fire. I seriously love sunsets and do not have a very good view of them where I live. But, I happened to look out my window just at the right time. The little part of the sky I could see was a brilliant red and pink. Someday, I really want to live in a cabin, or someplace that has a porch and deck, someplace to sit and see God's awesome sunsets. They are relaxing to me. I feel at peace and also in total awe at God's masterpieces, every day so different. No two sunsets the same—ever! Ever is a long time. From the very first sunset to the very last sunset on this Earth, no two are the same. It's just totally mind-boggling to me. And the sky is so huge! One thing I do like about Kansas is the huge prairie sky. And every sunrise and sunset is God's masterpiece, right there for everyone who is willing to notice. When I watch sunsets, I wonder what is going on in the world? Are people happy today? Did someone get married? Did someone have a baby? Or did someone lose a loved one to divorce or death? Did someone get that job they wanted? Did someone lose their job? Did someone get told they do not have any more cancer? Did someone get that dreaded cancer diagnosis? So many things happen to us every day—all day long. Do we ever stop and notice the sunsets and thank God for getting our attention? I've started wondering how many people God used, like he used Ron, to lead me back to Him--or better yet, used someone to tell someone about the Gospel who has never heard it before? How many people in one day, every day, get saved? I pray that number is mind-boggling, too. But, sunsets aren't the only beautiful sky moments. The clouds are amazing. They are constantly giving us glimpses of God's work. Do you ever think about all the clouds always moving, growing, and disappearing all day? Every day? I love watching thunderstorms build. Again, being in Kansas, you get a front-row seat to fantastic storm clouds, lightning, twisters, hail clouds, and then beautiful rainbows. And then the clear night sky? Especially a full moon, the harvest moon, the blue moon? The stars? The planets? The part that boggles my tiny brain is that it really looks like you can reach up and touch them. I can spend hours just looking at the sky. Can we really understand how far apart all the stars, sun, moon and planets are from us and from each other? I've read the number of miles, light years, but it just doesn't compute to me. Sometimes, just for fun, I put my finger up to a star or the moon. Like, there, I touched it! When I was little, I remember going home from my grandma and grandpa's farm, which took several hours. I remember watching out the window, when I wasn't sleeping, and watching the falling stars. And how did that moon know to follow us? I also remember telling my mom and dad that the sky looked like reverse chocolate chip ice cream. It made sense in my world! Chocolate chip ice cream is white with dark chips, so the reverse is dark sky with white stars. Totally makes sense to me!

So, back to my Bible study. This week's topic is evangelism. The thought of talking to someone about the Gospel scares the bejeebers out of me. I have family members and friends I have talked to God about. They don't want to hear it. Christian friends have told me that I must not be the one they need to hear it from. So, I constantly pray someone else will come alongside them and will share the Gospel in a way that they will listen and accept Jesus. I worry about their salvation. Every day, we hear about people we know, or someone famous, dying. My fear is that they will pass away and not be saved. Life is so short. We never know how long we are on this Earth. We are not promised tomorrow. Tomorrow is a gift, not an expectation. So, what if something unexpected and tragic happens and they never accepted Jesus? That thought breaks my heart. And, I don't understand how someone can look at a sunset, sunrise, or the heavens at night, and not believe it was created on purpose. Some people I know argue the scientific facts about how it all happened. I just can't convince them. So, talking about it is hard. But, I also know we are all commissioned to spread the Good News. We have to, or people won't know. And the awesome thing is that we don't all have to go to other countries to tell people. What about your neighbors? Co-workers? Friends? What about your family? I truly believe God put people in our lives either for us to bless them or them to be a blessing to us. But, do we ever think about that? Or do we just expect that people will always be in our lives and are there because we want them to be? God knows why everyone in your life is there. He knows about the people you see every day getting gas, eating out, shopping, or just doing life stuff. Think about all the people you see every day, even for a moment. Think about all the chances every day to find out if they believe or not. If so, awesome! If not, well, remember that God put that person and you in that moment. I hate rejection. I hate it when people want to argue about religion. It's about a personal relationship, not a religion. But, I don't feel like I know enough. I don't have the scriptures memorized. I don't think fast for good comebacks. So, when Ron and I took the Perspectives class, it really got in my brain that God commands us to tell people about Him. But, again, we don't have to be missionaries in third-world countries. There are ways, other than speaking. So, doing my Bible study about spreading God's Word made me think. Question #14 is "Are you confident that God has given you Acts 1:8 power? Why or why not?" According to my Bible, Acts 1:8 says "But, when the Holy Spirit has come upon you, you will receive power and will tell people about me everywhere, in Jerusalem, throughout Judea, in Samaria, and to the ends of the Earth". I do not think I am called to go to the ends of the Earth. But, I do believe God used Ron to lead me back to Him, and He used Ron's death to see that connection. I also believe that God is now using me to write this book to tell people about Him. I don't know where this book will end up…only in Topeka? In Kansas? Only in other states where my friends and family live and that's it? I hope not! Remember, I am a dreamer. I want this book somehow to tell people about how awesome God is, all over the place! People know people, who know people, who know people…yep, that's how the Gospel gets to the ends of the Earth. This book isn't just about Ron's life or my life. It's about what God did in Ron's life and is doing in my life and I hope and pray for what God will do and is doing in the life of whoever reads this book. I'm not a famous author. I'm not a theologian. I'm not anyone any better than anyone else. But, I love it that God uses ordinary people. The cool part is realizing when He is using you and then obeying. If Ron knew, he never told me, which I really believe he did, because he obeyed. Ron was big on obeying God. Sometimes, I really don't think Ron would have put up with me if he wasn't obeying God! I look back on how crazy and irrational and annoying I had to have been to him. I know I drove him crazy. I admit, sometimes I did it on purpose! Just to see that grin, his head shake, and see those beautiful eyes roll. And to hear his giggle. I loved his giggle. I really, really miss hearing that giggle. OK, back to obeying. Ron obeyed God…period. And, I believe God knows I am chicken to talk about Him to some people. But, I also believe God reminded me that way back when in junior high and high school, I always wanted to write a book. Not any novel or mystery or boring book. I loved creative writing. I didn't love all the rules, grammar, and stuff like that; it takes the love out of writing. So, when my pastor asked us all that one night how we were going to use our pain to help others and someone suggested writing this book, I truly believe God said, "Do this". So, I am. I am obeying. And, I am trusting that He will get this out to whoever he wants to read it. Whether it be to only family, friends and their friends, or to their friends and their families, and eventually to the ends of the Earth. This is all in God's hands. I'm just writing the thoughts He puts in my head. And I believe God has a sense of humor because He knows I love to talk and talk and talk. And He knows how long it takes me to tell what I want to say and He knows how long it takes me to get to the point. If I ever do get to the point, or even remember the point I started to make. So, God, being the awesome God He is in His sense of humor and being practical, figured a book is a great way to get my story out to people without subjecting them to having to listen to me go on and on and on. With this book, they can use a bookmark, close it and do something else, and come back to it. So, it's much better for me to write and ramble my thoughts and hopefully get it to more people than just by talking to them. And, better for you to read it. God knows what He's doing—He's God. And He constantly amazes me.

# March 11, 2014

This morning at women's Bible study, it was like God was giving me this information this morning to add more to what I wrote last night. Our speaker was so good! She talked about Luke 8:5-8. According to my Bible, those verses say (8:5) "A farmer went out to plant some seed. As he scattered it across his field, some seed fell on a footpath, where it was stepped on, and the birds came and ate it. (6) Other seed fell on shallow soil, with underlying rock. This seed began to grow, but soon it withered and died for lack of moisture. (7) Other seed fell among thorns that shot up and choked out the tender blades. (8) Still other seed fell on fertile soil. This seed grew and produced a crop one hundred times as much as had been planted." When He had said this, He called out, "Anyone who is willing to hear should listen and understand!"

So, when we talk to people about Jesus, or whoever is reading this, seeds are being planted. Then, we water the seeds with prayer. Offer to pray for that person, invite them to church, chat over coffee, anything—just plant the seed and water it. God does the rest! You may plant the seed, someone else may water it or harvest it, but God will do the work in that person. Maybe ask that person if they died tonight, are they certain they know if they will go to Heaven or hell. Tell them their works will not get them to Heaven. They have to believe and accept Jesus. You can pray the salvation prayer. This is what my Bible says about How We Can Know God:

## What's missing in our life?

Purpose, meaning, a reason for living—these are all things we desire and search for in life. But, despite our search, we still feel empty and unfulfilled. We each have an empty place in our hearts, a spiritual void, a "God-shaped vacuum" (Ecclesiastes 2:24-25). Possessions won't fill it, nor will success, relationships, or even religion. Only through a vibrant relationship with God can this void be filled. But, before such a relationship can be established, we need to face a serious problem.

## The Problem: Sin

The Bible identifies this problem as sin. Sin is not just the bad things we do, but an inherent part of who we are. We are not sinners because we sin; we sin because we are sinners. King David wrote "I was born a sinner—yes, from the moment my mother conceived me" (Psalm 51:5). Because we are born sinners, sinning comes to us naturally. Scripture tells us "the human heart is most deceitful and desperately wicked. Who really knows how bad it is?" (Jeremiah 17:9). Every problem we experience in society today can be traced back to our refusal to live God's way.

## The Solution: Jesus Christ

God understood our problem and knew we could not beat it alone. So, He lovingly sent His own Son, Jesus Christ, to bridge the chasm of sin that separates us from God (Romans 3:22). Jesus laid aside His divine privileges and walked the Earth as a man, experiencing all the troubles and emotions that we do. Then, He was arrested on false charges and killed on a Roman cross. But, this was no accident. He did it to suffer the punishment deserved by us all. And then, three days later, Jesus rose from the dead, conquering sin and death forever!

## The Response: Accepting God's Offer

To know Jesus Christ personally and have our sins forgiven, we must first believe that we are sinners separated from God and that our only hope is Jesus Christ, the Son of God, Who came to Earth and died for our sins (Acts 3:19). But, we must not stop with this realization. We also need to take steps toward confessing and turning from our sins. We must welcome Jesus Christ into our life as Lord and Savior. He will move in and help us to change from the inside out.

If you are ready to repent of your sins and believe in Jesus Christ so that you can receive His forgiveness, take a moment to pray like this:

"God, I'm sorry for my sins. Right now, I turn from my sins and ask You to forgive me. Thank You for sending Jesus Christ to die on the cross for my sins. Jesus, I ask You to come into my life and be my Lord, Savior and Friend. Thank You for forgiving me eternal life. In Jesus' Name, I pray. Amen"

If you prayed this prayer and meant it, you can be sure that God has forgiven you and received you into His family. It would be good to tell a friend, possibly a pastor, about your new decision to let Jesus be the Lord of your life. As a new Christian, you will also want to find a Bible-believing church, where you can meet together with other believers. They can encourage you and help you grow in your new faith.

All this is from my Bible—a simple to read and understand Bible called The Book. A friend recommended it to me and now I am passing on to you that it has helped me so much in my Bible studies and daily journaling.

And all I can say is "wow"! I totally had no thought or plan to include this part in my book. The thought never crossed my mind. I don't know it all or have it all memorized or feel qualified to lead others to Christ. But, remember how I said that God uses ordinary people all the time? Well, God put the Bible study, the speaker, and the homework together last night. And He put all that in my mind and wrote those words on this paper. It's all God, not me. I'm just obeying. I pray that someone reading this felt something. That a light bulb came on or made you think a little bit. If you are already a believer, that's awesome. If you aren't, please ask yourself this question: If you died tonight, do you know where you will spend eternity? Heaven or Hell? It's totally your choice.

# MARCH 22, 2014

So, tonight after church, my father-in-law introduced me to this man who has published six books! He gave me some good advice about how to get this published! There is an Authors Club here in town that meets the third Saturday of every month. He said someone there would love to read all of this and give me an opinion, advice, etc. I'm pretty excited! I really hope I can understand the Create Space he told me about—how to go online and self-publish. He said this Club has been around since the early 1900's. That's a long time! That's a lot of experiences people had to pass on to others. He said most people are his age—70's—and they would love new, young blood in their group! What an honor to be invited to a group with so much knowledge. I just now pray that they will like this and believe that you will, too! Anyone can self-publish. Lots of people do it all the time. The online books, e-readers, and so on, seem to be better than book stores. We will see! If you are reading this, then thank you and I pray you enjoy it and recommend it to others! But, please warn others, as I forgot to warn you in the beginning, that if you are one of those people who require grammatical correctness, this book will be frustrating to you and drive you crazy! I don't have a clue how to write like that. It's not who I am. I write like I think, and I do not think grammatically correct.

One week later...got to church and one of Ron's parents' friends told me that the man I met last week has some books for me! How awesome is that?! The thin paperback I read in a few hours. It's called "Self-publishing Planning for a Better Book" by Roger Lloyd Williams.

The cool thing is it is published by Mennonite Press in Newton, KS, which is only a couple of hours down the interstate. Who woulda thunk it? God did! The other book is a hardback called "Beginning Writer's Answer Book" by Kirk Polking and the editors of Writer's Digest. This book is thicker and full of things I didn't think about or even know I was supposed to think about. Not everything pertained to my situation, but I learned a lot and am very grateful for God putting this man and his wife in my life!

Sundays are the hardest, especially since football season is over. The basketball tournament is on, but I'm not into basketball that much. I watched my K-State team, but they got knocked out already; so did KU—not that I like KU, or Wichita, who also got beat today, but at least they were Kansas teams. Sundays are hard because Ron isn't here. It seemed like a very, very long day today. I did stuff, took a nap, walked my dogs, ran some errands, and today isn't over yet! I kept wanting to write today, but God didn't tell me what to write. I never really think about what to write. God always tells me. Sometimes, I really don't understand His timing! At 8:30 p.m., I was in my kitchen for a minute, which is all I ever am in my kitchen. I looked at my kitchen table. That was it. I need to write about my kitchen table. It's just there. I never eat there anymore—ever. When I have family here and actually feed them, they sit there, but not me. I look at where Ron sat. Sometimes, it's just stupid, simple things like his chair at the table that makes me really miss him. I remember when we did eat at the table. It wasn't all the time. Wanna know why? Well, cause remember I told you I am a "stuff" person? Well, I always had piles of stuff on the table. I know that bothered him. Now, I am trying to not keep so much stuff on it. But, without stuff, it looks bare, boring, lonely. Sometimes, I'd move the stuff so we could eat there. Usually, we sat on the couch and ate on his two wooden TV trays. Ron didn't have a kitchen table, so he was used to not eating at one. So, now, I eat at his wooden TV tray. He had two of them. One I use to eat on; the other one is beside his comfy chair that I always sit in. Piled on that TV tray are my Bibles, Bible study book, Jesus Calling devotional, Bible daily journal, and this notebook. So, yes, it's covered. But, covered with good things. I live in this chair.

So, it makes sense that my Bibles, journal, and this notebook should be right beside it, so it's right there when I need them. Which is always! On the other TV tray I eat on is my Max Lucado devotional calendar a good friend gave me after Ron passed away. Every morning when I sit down to eat, I read what Max Lucado has to say that day. Then, on the other tray is Jesus Calling. I read those before I eat. Sometimes, I will type one or the other and post on Facebook. Kinda my way of spreading God's Word, like we are commanded. Then, I usually do my daily journal my church does together. Each day has a verse or several verses to read. Then, we are to write what stuck out to us. I don't always get it done first thing, but I try. At small group, we go over the prior week's reading. It's just making myself be disciplined to do it first thing, rather than a bunch of days at once or at the last minute before group. Between women's morning Bible study and small group in the evening, I know I'm to be in the Word daily. To give my first and my best, not my last and my leftovers. Ron was so good at faithfully giving God his first and his best. I am trying. I feel much better when I start my days out with God. I really wish Ron knew I was paying attention to his faithfulness to God. I also wish I would have been better at it then, so Ron would have been proud of me. He never said anything, though. It makes sense to me, though—God was using him in so many ways to teach me about Him. He just quietly did what God told him—he was available and obedient to God. It's funny, though. I used to always do my journal and Bible studies at the kitchen table. There was room enough for that. I really wish I would have kept the table clear back then. He would have liked that. Now, it's clear and he isn't here. It's just empty, bare, boring, and lonely. Kind of how I feel right now. Empty, bare, boring, and lonely.

# April 4, 2014

Tonight was amazing. Catacombs was about three and a half hours of intense study of the arrest, crucifixion, and resurrection of Jesus. Our amazing youth pastor led the class and our awesome worship leader led worship. I learned so much through this in-depth study. I really wish more people would have come. Many believers, particularly in the underground movement in Asia, gather like this. I looked up the word "catacombs". It says catacombs are human-made subterranean passageways for religious practice. Tonight, it was held in the basement in a very special room. It's called the Children's Theater. It's special to me because that's mainly where Ron served in Tech Arts. He did the sound and video for the children's program, worship, and On Belay, which included parents. It's special also because this is the room Ron dearly loved, and where his visitation was held. After Ron passed away, it took me a long time to be able to go downstairs. In the basement is also where the fellowship hall is located. In the fellowship hall Tuesday morning women's Bible study is held. Also, it's where volunteers rotate cooking supper every Saturday between the two services. When Ron would serve in the Children's Theater, I would attend service upstairs. We would then eat supper and I would hang out with him while he served during the second service. That's a pretty special room. Volunteers made a lunch for friends and family after Ron's service. That was horribly hard, going downstairs and eating without him. The two rooms are very close together. The bathrooms are very close, too. The Children's Theater is at the bottom of the steps and right next to the elevator. The only way to go downstairs and not go by or see the Children's Theater is to use the back door. The back door is just steps away from the fellowship hall. Totally hard to avoid those two rooms. But, those rooms are the only reasons I need to go downstairs. It took me awhile to be able to go down and attend Bible study. I remember one time right after I returned to Bible study, I was going to the bathroom and stopped dead in my tracks. I was right in front of the Children's Theater. I pressed my face up to the glass and burst into tears. It was dark and empty. But, I could see the screens where his video was for his visitation. I saw the tech booth where he served with a passion. It broke my heart. I could hear the youth worship band playing so loud and the little kids singing along. I could hear the youth pastor giving his message. Even though that room was now dark and quiet, all those noises and memories came flooding back in a flash. I couldn't stop sobbing. Friends came over and hugged me, comforted me, and some even cried with me. I hate crying in front of others, but I couldn't stop. The thought that Ron would never be running sound and video in that booth again broke my heart. Just remembering that moment makes me cry as I am writing this. Grief is so hard! Eventually, I could walk by there. It took awhile, but I did it. It also took a long time to be able to eat there again. I still will not eat there alone. Back to tonight and Catacombs. Tonight, a friend from small group went with me. I would not have gone alone. Besides my friend, I only knew the youth pastor, worship leader, my small group leader and husband, and a couple of other people. On our first break, my friend left to get home before dark. I felt a little lost at first, but the message was so powerful that it kept my attention. Every once in awhile, I would catch myself thinking "I am sitting alone in this room and I am OK". I wished Ron was sitting with me, but I truly felt his presence sitting in my friend's seat. It felt good tonight to listen, learn, and worship in a room full of memories and feel at peace and be able to smile. God is good! Last night when I felt Ron sit down in the chair beside me after my friend left, it was so peaceful. Something has been nagging at me for about 6-8 months and I didn't know what to do about it. Kind of an inner turmoil at times. I have been feeling a tug to go back to the place where Ron and I went on our honeymoon. We didn't have much money, so we couldn't go on any big, fancy or long trip. Those who know me know I don't do fancy. Not even close! Ron found this place called The Elms Hotel in Excelsior Springs, Missouri. I never heard of the town or the hotel. Excelsior Springs is 25 miles northeast of Kansas City, MO. It is a small town with lots of artsy life. I immediately fell in love with it. It was July and very hot and muggy, but that didn't stop us, even though I despise the temperature over 75 degrees. It's nestled in lush trees and hills and just a very cute town. We only got to stay two nights. We said we would go back. It never happened. When we got to town, we turned this corner, and wow! The Elms Resort and Spa was huge! It looked amazing and we weren't even there yet. Inside, I'm sure I was a spectacle, walking around with my mouth open. I had never been anyplace so fancy before. Like I said, I don't do fancy! It is more than 125 years old and all restored beautifully. It sits on 16 acres of awesomeness. Again, so lush and peaceful. There is a restaurant, spa, you name it—The Elms has it! Our room was one of the old ones. It was beautiful. Ron told me that Al Capone and President Harry Truman stayed there a lot. Truman stayed at The Elms the night of the 1948 election. Wow, so much history is mind-boggling, especially for my tiny mind. So, after we unloaded our stuff...OK, my stuff, since Ron wasn't a stuff person. Poor guy. This was when he discovered I had to bring close to everything I owned just for two nights. I justified how it all made sense in my world. We asked the guy at the desk where the best place in town to eat was. He said the Wabash Blues Garden. It was just a short walk. Wabash is an old historic train depot. A small place, but we could tell it's a favorite cause it was packed. It is a BBQ place and has live entertainment in spring through fall. It just so happened there was a band that evening outside. It was a blues band that was obviously a favorite local band since it seemed a lot of people knew the band members. I was in heaven. Even though it was a zillion degrees, even in the evening, and a bazillion degrees humidity, I had a blast. We checked out the hot tub...what a way to relax after an amazing day. The guy at the desk also told us about a place to eat breakfast. The Mill Inn Restaurant had excellent French toast and the best service ever. It was a little mom and pop place that was so cozy and friendly. Our waitress talked and talked and really made us feel welcome. Then, we were off to Excelsior Springs Hall of Water Museum. I was very interested in learning about the mineral springs and hoping to get some relief for my fibromyalgia. You can look up the history if you want, just trust me—it's very interesting all the people who used to go there to be healed and drink mineral water from the water bar. The history and décor of this museum is very much worth your time to Google or visit in person. We ate lunch at Ray's Lunch and Diner. Oh, this place is special! It's very tiny, and is all decked out in 50's style. There are 45's all over the wall and all kinds of memorabilia on the walls. The menu is on a board behind the counter. We were told they are famous for their chili and cinnamon rolls. Ron loved chili, tried it and loved it. And those cinnamon rolls? The best ever! Ray knows a tourist when he sees one. He asked us questions, talked a lot, and took our picture outside the diner. Evidently, he does this all the time. He had it down. He and his staff were so friendly. We said we had to come back to this town, just to go eat there. Again, we never made it back. We spent the day wandering through the little shops and did the art walk, which was a blast. We had never been to an art walk before. Being the dreamer that I am, I spent a ton of money thinking about how this piece would be awesome, we couldn't possibly live without this or that, or oh, look at this! Poor Ron. Good thing we didn't have the money for all the cool things I found or we would have needed a U-Haul to get home. Remember, Ron wasn't a "stuff" person. He would just smile and roll his eyes. I'm sure he was secretly wondering what in the world did he get himself into and how was he gonna ever figure this kooky lady out? Besides being a dreamer, I love nature. I am at peace when I am in nature. At The Elms, I talked him into exploring the huge acreage and walk this trail I discovered. I had no clue where it went or how long it was, but it was a walking trail so it wasn't out in the wilderness or anything. So, Ron being Ron, went along with my adventure idea. I don't remember how far we walked. I do remember it was a long ways. And remember I told you, it is a hilly town? Well, whoever made that trail sure made it a point to go up and down, up and down, winding through woody parts, through parts of the town by The Elms. I was sure we had walked miles and miles and miles. At least, it felt like it! And I also am a photo-bug. Not a pro. Don't even own a camera. Then, I had to use the disposable ones. Boy, did I go through those! I can take 100 pictures of the same thing, but at different angles. Ron really wasn't into nature or caring about capturing pictures of everything we saw in a zillion different ways. But, Ron was a patient man and, again, was probably wondering what he got himself into. I could not understand how someone would not want a ton of pictures of the same thing at different angles. It did not make a bit of sense to me. We ate supper in the restaurant at The Elms. Remember I told you I'm not a fancy person? Well, this restaurant was very fancy…at least to me it was. The food was good, but I liked the little mom and pop places we ate at better. I fit in much better. After relaxing in the hot tub again that evening, sitting outside, I just looked at the huge hotel and thought about all the history, all the people who had stayed there, over more than 125 years. Of course, I babbled on and on to Ron about how cool the history was and how I didn't want to leave the next day to get back to reality. Ron was a reality person. He was not a dreamer at all. I cannot understand people who don't dream. Reality is a necessity, I know, but why be in it all the time if you don't have to be? Why not dream? This world would be a very boring place without dreamers. We are needed in this world! Some of us are just a little more out of touch with reality than others, but that's OK! After eating yummy French toast for breakfast the next morning, we were off, back to that reality stuff again. Ron promised we would come back sometime for some anniversary or special occasion. Never happened. On the way home, we stopped at Tryst Park, which had a beautiful waterfall, and The James Farm, which is a preserved farmhouse where Jesse James was born in 1847. It has an audio-visual presentation of the history of Frank and Jesse James. There are artifacts, the house, and the original burial site of Jesse James. Again, what would take normal people less time to walk through took us longer because of having to take so many pictures of the same thing! Oh, yeah, the gift shop was awesome, too! I loved the history and learned a lot. It isn't even that far from home, but I had no clue this place existed. Or that the cute little town of Excelsior Springs existed. A whole nother world just so close to home.

So, back to my inner nagging. I've been wanting to go back to that town, The Elms, the mom and pop places, the shops, the memories. I feel a tug to go. I don't want to go alone, but would anyone else appreciate those places and their meaning to me? What if whoever I convinced to join me found those places boring? I don't understand how anyone would or could, but that's just me. Or, do I go by myself? That scares the bejeebers out of me. But, is that what I need to do? To have that silence? To have those memories, just to myself? I don't know what to do. I don't know why there is this tug to go back. Is it a God thing? Is He telling me I need to go? Why would He do that? Why would He want me to be in that cool little town without Ron? Why would He want me to have all those memories come flooding back again? Why would He put me through that? I don't know. Maybe that's why I have been ignoring this tug for awhile. Could it be that I am writing this today, after feeling Ron sit by me last night when my friend left? I felt peace then. So, now that I felt that peace, why did I decide this morning I need to spill my guts and write about it now? Is it that it's reassurance that I need to go and that I will be OK? If it's a God thing, I can't ignore it and not be obedient and not go. This July 7, 2014 will be seven years ago that we were there on our honeymoon. It just dawned on me that when we got married on 7-7-07 that tons of other people did, too, because it was considered lucky. Hmmm… lucky? Doesn't seem lucky to me that four years after getting married, God took Ron away from me. If we are going with the number seven being lucky and this July will be seven years, maybe I should go. Really, though, how can I go on luck when I have God? Duh… I may be slow, but as I'm writing this, it's showing me that this is a no-brainer. I gotta go. The question is, do I go alone and keep those memories to myself, or do I take someone along and share those memories? God will tell me what to do. He always does. I just have to listen and obey. I don't have a clue how I will afford it or get there, but God does.

# April 6, 2014

I just thanked God again for using Ron to lead me, kicking and screaming, from Manhattan to here, to FBC, to this incredible body of people who I love so much and appreciate all they do. Every time I go there, it is truly a family reunion. Without Ron being available and obedient to God, I am sure I would still be living in Manhattan, close to my family, but very lonely, very sad, very broken, and very far away from God. I always believed in God. I always prayed. I always talked to God. But, I didn't always KNOW God. I didn't know about a relationship with God. I didn't know a lot of things I know now. There are lots more things I still don't know, may never know. But, I do know that God used Ron, an ordinary guy. I know that somehow God is using me and will continue to use me. I just have to have open ears, eyes, mind, and heart to hear, see, and obey God. I may not ever understand, this side of Heaven, why things happen. But, God knows. He knows the story; He wrote it. He knows the joy, fears, struggles, tears, laughter, pain, love, anxiety, and excitement. He knows the ending. All I have to do is obey and trust, sit back and hold on, and let Him be in the driver's seat.

# APRIL 8, 2014

Writing is therapy for me and just like how this book began by that question "How are you going to use this pain to help someone else?", "God doesn't waste a hurt", and "someday, someone in Heaven may come up to you and thank you for them being there". So, somehow, I hope this pain can help someone out there…even one person, a tiny bit. Let's just say since I learned about my nephew's death, I was very concerned about his salvation. I know it's between him and God. God knows the answer. All I can do is pray. I pray for my family members who do not know Jesus, who don't believe in Him. I want to make them believe, but I can't. I can plant seeds and pray a lot. God does the rest. I'm not God, and I can't do His job. Sometimes, I just don't understand why things happen. Why? Why? Why? God knows. I worry about my family and friends who do not believe. As with my parents, Ron, my grandparents, brother-in-law, and other loved ones who have passed without any warning, some may not have believed. We never know how much time we have on this Earth. Some people have time toward the end to repent; others don't. I cannot stand the thought of not seeing my friends and family in Heaven. I think some people just assume that when everyone dies, they automatically go to Heaven. Only God knows their final destination. I just can't understand why some people want to take that chance?

I know bad things happen to make us open our eyes and think. "And we know God causes everything to work together for the good of those who love God and are called according to His purpose for them"

(Romans 8:28). "Can anything ever separate us from Christ's love? Does it mean He no longer loves us if we have trouble or calamity, or are persecuted, or are hungry or cold or in danger or threatened with death?" (Romans 9:35). "And I am convinced that nothing can ever separate us from His love. Death can't and life can't. The angels can't and the demons can't. Our fears for today, our worries about tomorrow, and even the powers of hell can't keep God's love away. Whether we are high above the sky or in the deepest ocean, nothing in all Creation will ever be able to separate us from the love of God that is revealed in Christ Jesus our Lord" (Romans 9:38-39).

Wow. Just like before, I had no thoughts or plans to write more scripture. None. God led me to them. I can't top this. I also cannot explain the incredible peace I felt writing these words and reading them after I wrote them. It's an amazing feeling. I pray that if you don't know or feel this peace that you decide you want peace over worry or despair or anything else. That you want to feel peace and love. God's love. That out of this sad tragedy of losing my hubby, that somehow, some way, this will help someone out there to get curious and search and find and believe. It blows my mind the words God puts on paper through my pen. It's all from Him. I don't think about what I write; it just happens. I cannot imagine grieving this death without my faith. I had to with my dad's death in 1998 and it was horrible, agonizing, relentless pain that never ended. I can tell my faith has grown since my mom's death in 2009 to Ron's death in 2011. But, it has soared so high after Ron's death. I'm still a newbie. I don't have it all figured out. I don't understand it all—not even close. And it took losing Ron for that faith to grow more. And, as much as it hurts to not have Ron here on this Earth with us anymore, I know God had and has a plan. Thank You God, again, for using Ron.

One of my very favorite verses: "For I know the plans I have for you, says the Lord. They are plans for good and not for disaster, to give you a future and a hope. In those days when you pray, I will listen. If you look for Me in earnest you will find Me when you seek Me" (Jeremiah 29:11-13). I loved this verse so much that we used it at Ron's service. I also made it into my e-mail address: sdjeremiah2911@gmail.com.

Well, I guess I'm not done writing for tonight. The previous part about my nephew I started writing at 1:25 a.m. I wrote until 3:08 a.m., then took the dogs out one more time, and we were going to bed. I was almost in bed and then it's "Nope, you're not done yet". Really? You're kidding, right? Remember when I talked about God's timing when He told me to write about the kitchen table at 8:30 p.m. and I kinda grumbled? I am a night owl. I always have been and most of my family are, too. But, seriously? It's 4:15 a.m.! That's AM, as in I have to be up at 8:00 AM. I don't do mornings very well and never have. But, getting up in the morning…nope, not for me. I love that saying that says "I'd love mornings better if they happened later in the day", or something like that. I don't remember how it goes, exactly. I'm tired. My head hurts. I feel exhausted, physically and emotionally. With fibro, it doesn't take much to make me tired. So, here I am writing. Because I'm supposed to. So, I will. You know what? Ron wasn't perfect. Know what else? I'm not either. Know what else? You aren't either. We never will be. We can't be. I know it sounds like I made Ron out to be a saint so far. But, he wasn't. I'm not either. We're human. We're broken. We all are. Ron could be stubborn. So can I. Sometimes, two stubborn people don't always agree on things. Sometimes, we each wanted our way. And since Ron was the practical, realistic person and I am the "it all makes sense in my world" dreamer, obviously we didn't always think alike. Sometimes, we had disagreements. Sometimes, we fought. Sometimes, it seemed like the fighting would never end. I'm a crier. I cry about everything and everything makes me cry. Always been that way. When my mother unexpectedly passed away in 2009, it broke my heart. I cried and I cried and I cried. I remember sometimes Ron would tell me, "It's been a year now; why are you still crying?" He didn't get it. He couldn't get it. He didn't lose his mom. I'm very thankful she's here with me. But, until you lose a mom, you don't understand. You can't. Sometimes, I couldn't understand how there were any tears left in me to cry. I didn't have a clue that a year later, I would say the same thing when Ron passed away.

Back to fighting. I think my mom passing away threw me into a deep depression. My pastor recommended a therapist who I dearly love and happens to go to our church. I went for awhile, then when I quit my job as a para because of fibro, I lost my insurance until I was on disability. During that 'no insurance' time, I went to a Christian counseling place that went by our income. They didn't get rich from us, that's for sure. I'm back to seeing her again.

We kept fighting, so Ron got counseling on his own. I'm surprised he didn't need it way before then, as crazy as I drove him! Then, we had counseling together. We were on counseling overload. Sometimes, we left feeling great and glad we went. Sometimes, we left more confused, sad, mad, and all those other things, than when we went in. We tried really hard not to go to sleep angry. Sometimes it worked; sometimes the sun rose and we were still talking. That was amazing because Ron was very much a routine person. Bedtime was after the news and weather and ice cream. Chocolate, of course. Death by Chocolate. With lots of Hershey's syrup. That's what he liked, so I dished it up for him every night at 10:00.

We really tried our hardest to live by the verse "And don't sin by letting anger gain control over you. Don't let the sun go down while you are still angry, for anger gives a mighty foothold to the Devil." (Ephesians 4:26-27). Satan had a blast with that one. We could hear him laughing. I'm not gonna give the gory details of our fights. I didn't even want to write about this. It's ugly. It's painful, it's embarrassing, and it's important. It's important because we all have skeletons. And Satan thoroughly enjoys opening the gate and watching them try to defeat us. But, you know what? It didn't happen. God defeated Satan. But, Satan tried really hard to destroy us. Those whispers of doubt. Those "what if's?" Those "if only…". Those "if he really loved you…" And on and on. We discussed divorce. We didn't want it. Sometimes, it just seemed like we were too tired and weary to keep trying. Sometimes, Satan was very close to winning. But, he didn't. And if he had won, Ron's and my story would have ended differently. Then I wouldn't be writing this. I wouldn't have had this whole experience since he passed away on October 2, 2011. We weren't perfect. We were sinners. I am a sinner. Jesus was the only perfect One. The only One Who didn't sin. The One Who had to die for our sins. We all have skeletons. We get hurt; we hurt others. Forgiveness is hard, very hard, sometimes. But, we have to do it. It doesn't mean we are saying what the person did to hurt us, or vice versa, was OK. It means it frees us. We are commanded to forgive. God forgave us. We are all sinners. We aren't perfect, and never can be. Stop trying; it's not gonna happen.

"Where is another God like You, Who pardons the sins of the survivors among His people? You cannot stay angry with Your people forever, because You delight in showing mercy. Once again, You will have compassion on us. You will trample our sins under your feet and throw them into the depths of the ocean! You will show us Your faithfulness and unfailing love as You promised with an oath to our ancestors Abraham and Jacob long ago" (Micah 7:18-19). Wow. I have never read this before right now.

And "But, when you are praying, first forgive anyone you are holding a grudge against, so that your Father in Heaven will forgive your sins, too" (Mark 11:25).

And, lastly…Matthew 6:9-15:

"Pray like this: Our Father, Who art in heaven, hallowed be Your Name, Your kingdom come, Your will be done on Earth as it is in Heaven. Give us this day our daily bread. Forgive us our trespasses as we forgive those who trespass against us. And lead us not into temptation, but deliver us from evil. For Thine is the kingdom, the power, and the glory forever and ever. Amen".

Wow. I'm going to bed now. It's 5:25 AM. Good night, world… or good morning…

# April 9, 2014

Wow, no rest for me. It was 6:00 a.m. when I got to bed. The alarm went off at 8:00 a.m. I love my sleep—like 8-10-12 hours of sleep. Two isn't enough. I told myself "it's OK, I'll take a nap this afternoon". I went to my 10:00 a.m. therapy appointment. Boy, did I need it! Having a female Christian therapist is awesome, especially from my church!

So, afterwards, I go get food for my puppies. My plan was to take them potty and curl up on the loveseat for a good nap with them. Naps with my dogs rate up close to the top of my favorite ways to relax and de-stress. So, after getting dog food, I start home and I'm not supposed to come home. Cemetery. But, why? I haven't been there for awhile, but I only go when I feel I'm supposed to. OK, good thing it's not too far out of the way, really. Not far from my church. I drove up, got out, walked across the road. The cemetery is outside of town a little. It's on a little hill, kind of. It's beautiful and peaceful. Would be better without the interstate right beside it, but, oh, well. I can't move it. Our grave is under this cool tree. Being in Kansas, it's always windy. The shade and wind made it a little chilly. I thought "Ron would be freezing". Yep, he would be cold. I got to wondering why grass hasn't grown over his grave yet. It's been two and a half years and it's still dirt. Then, I looked good at the stone. It was dirty. The last time I was there, it was covered in snow. Ron definitely would not like that! Ron was a clean freak. Well, actually, he was probably pretty normal. No, he wasn't; he was a clean freak. He was meticulous. So, I went over and got napkins out of my glove box. My mom taught me to keep them there. You never know when you might need them. Ron always gave me a hard time about them. He tolerated them, but if he needed something from the glove box, he had to deal with napkins. I had fun with this one! Ha! His stone was dirty and I was prepared with my napkins to wipe it clean. So, there, Ron! Got him back! I really enjoy these moments! I know he was grinning, shaking his head, and rolling those eyes. I'd give anything to see that in person again. I thought a few minutes, remembering the tent that was there two and a half years ago. I remembered sitting there with Ron's mom and dad, my family, and Ron's family. I remembered looking behind me and seeing a lot of people. Some I didn't know. Most were crying or talking. Yeah, the wind was blowing that day, too. Of course it was; this is Kansas! I looked at the stone. Praying hands on the top corners of his side and my side and a wedding ring in the middle with our wedding date. Then, the birth and death dates of Ron. My birth date. What's written underneath all that, centered, says "Walking With Jesus". That always makes me smile. I look up in the sky and smile again. This grave is just where his shell is. A place for his loved ones to come say "hi". I always say "hi, whatcha doing?" Duh, I know what he's doing. He's walking with Jesus. I can't wait to walk with Jesus!

I get home, tend to the dogs, planning on taking my nap now. Nope, not yet. I was told to write this all down first. Really? Again? I honestly thought I was done writing for a few days or at least a few more hours! I'm tired; I want a nap! Can't I write later? God gives me the words anyway. Nope. Gotta write now. So, I did. Who am I to argue and say no to God? NOW, I'm taking a nap! Later, gater…

# April 15, 2014

Yesterday, I spent two and a half hours at Lifeway, looking for Bibles for my granddaughters, 16 and 11, for Easter. They have Bibles that others gave them, but they are complicated and I want them to be able to understand what they read. I want them to want to learn more about God, what He tells us to do, how to live, how to love, what is right, what is wrong, and Who He is and why they should believe in Him, love Him, and obey Him. They are pretty new in this journey and I firmly believe that some way, somehow, I am to be a part of helping them all I can to know Christ. I don't know it all; I don't even know a lot. But, what I do know is this: that the little bit I know is enough that it totally changed my life and has made me want to learn more, and try to wrap my tiny brain around how big God is and how deep and wide His love is for us. Not just the smart ones, best looking ones, rich ones, popular ones, but each one of us. He made us, each of us, in His image—so, why wouldn't He love us? In this broken world we live in, we are used to people stop loving us. If we mess up, if we don't mess up. Sometimes, just because they want to stop loving us—no good reason. So, we are used to that threat of losing someone's love. We can't lose God's love. We can't. It can't happen. No matter how hard we try, because we may feel we don't deserve His love. So, we may run away. But, we can't hide—duh—He's God and He knows all and sees all. We can't hide and He doesn't want us to.

So, I decided that since it's almost Easter, that it's a perfect time to give them new Bibles that fit who they are and where they are in this journey. Yeah, two and a half hours for two Bibles and two Bible covers. So many to choose from. I would get it narrowed down and then spy one I overlooked. The lady who helped me was so nice. She spent a lot of time helping me, answering my questions, trying to help me find the perfect Bibles and covers. I about fell over at the register, but these are investments in their lives, in their salvations. So, it's totally worth it. I just pray they are as excited as I am!

A couple of weeks ago at Thursday night small group, a friend gave me a small journal for my granddaughter. I had shared the week before about some concerns I had for them and wanted to somehow make finding verses easier when they need them. So, also yesterday, I got another small journal and spent hours writing down Bible verses that I felt are really important to each one at this time. Then, I wrote the Ten Commandments, The Lord's Prayer, The Golden Rule, and many other verses in these journals. I spent most of today finishing up. That's a lot of writing! In the front, I wrote their name, from me, and the date they will get them. After all the verses I wrote the same, I wrote a personal note to each one, saying why I was doing this, and explaining the verses I picked that were just for them individually. Correction...I didn't pick them. God told me which ones to write the same and individually. Since their ages are different, their journeys are different. All of our journeys are different. Each one has different "stuff" in their life that I pray these verses will help with and teach them and comfort them. Then, there are a lot of blank pages for them to hopefully someday write down their own favorite Bible verses. I pray they keep these and read them over and over and cherish them for many years. They may not understand how important those verses and all of God's words are right now, but I am going to do my best to introduce them to a relationship and let God do the rest. I can't make anyone be interested or decide to know Jesus. Sometimes, I wish I could make people understand. But, all I can do is plant the seeds, pray a lot, and let God do His work.

And the coolest part? That this would never have happened if God hadn't used Ron. If Ron never gave me my Bible for our first Christmas. If Ron hadn't ever invited me to FBC. If Ron hadn't listened and obeyed. If God hadn't given me Ron for four years, then taken him away from me, his parents, his family and friends. If God hadn't had this all figured out—the beginning, the journey I am on now--and God knows how it's gonna end. He's the author—He knows. If none of that happened, then I wouldn't be here writing all this now. Writing what God tells me to write. It may sound weird, but trust me, these are not my words. They are His words being written like how I talk.

I'm so very thankful God used Ron. I'm glad Ron obeyed. I'm not glad God took Ron away. Why couldn't God have written this story differently so I could still have Ron, and Ron still led me to FBC and Him? I don't understand why I couldn't have both? Have Ron here and my relationship with God. But, who am I to tell God how to write His story? God has this all figured out. I just have to believe and trust. And be thankful. Thankful for the happy times, the sad times, the love, the struggles, the tears, the pain, the laughs, the people in my life, and the people He had in my life who aren't here anymore. I don't understand why people were in and out of my life when I didn't want them to leave. But, God put them all there for a reason. He put the people who are in my life now for a reason. He will continue to put people in and out of my life as long as I am on this Earth. Even though I don't understand it all, I am still thankful.

I pray someday my granddaughters will look back at Easter 2014 and remember the new Bibles and the journals, just for them, and be thankful.

God is good.

# April 16, 2014

What an amazing birthday!!! Ron's mom and dad took me to brunch at Cracker Barrel, then we went to the 1:00 p.m. opening of Heaven Is For Real. They are the best in-laws on this planet! God gave me the best second set of parents, hands down! They are so kind, supportive, compassionate, loving, and there are not enough words known to man to describe them. For those of you reading this who know them, you know what I mean. They are also so cute together. They make me smile. They also make me laugh. I am so blessed that God put them in my life. If only there were a way to clone them, the world would be a much better place. But, God didn't do that. I hope they realize how much I love and respect them.

Brunch was yummy, as always. I love Cracker Barrel! I only eat the Momma's French Toast and raspberry tea. Yummy, yummy. The waitress was rude, though. It was so good to have that time with them to talk and laugh. It meant so very much to me.

We went to the theater early, expecting a line since today was opening day. Our church had the Burpos come to Topeka to TPAC a couple of years ago. My kids, a friend, and I went to listen to them. I sent the kids' version of the book to my granddaughters for Christmas. I did not read the adult book, though. The movie was very good. I was disappointed that there were not many people there. I hope it was just because it was 1:00 p.m. on a Wednesday. I teared up quite a few times. I didn't need the Kleenex I figured I would need. My father-in-law even went and bought Kleenex before going to the theater. Is that love or what?! I'm not going to tell about the movie, only that I thought it was very good and I highly recommend it.

Then, at 6:00 p.m., I went to the Passion Play with two friends from my Thursday night small group. I'd never been to see it before. One of my friends saw it several times; my other friend never had been to it before either. All I could say was "wow". Each act was "wow". I loved the songs, too. It seemed so real. The crucifixion was very loud, heartbreaking, and so real. You could feel his pain when being whipped and then nailed to the cross. That made me cry. But, the best part? When he appeared to Mary at the tomb and his followers learned he was alive. It was the best couple of hours ever. Afterwards, there were people to come to talk to you if you had questions, needed prayer, or just needed to talk to someone about what just happened. I wish other people I know would go see it. But, I cannot make them. The cast was huge! They were all in the lobby afterwards to greet and talk to people. I got to see Jesus up close! I cannot wait! It really made me think about how amazing it's going to be in Heaven with Jesus, disciples, and loved ones. I must confess I'm jealous that Ron and my loved ones are already there! But, I know there is some reason God wants me on this Earth longer. I just wish He would hurry up and come back!

I miss Ron and my mom and dad every day, but more so on my birthday and holidays. I love and miss them so much. I'm sure they were all smiling down at today's events. I'm very thankful I didn't have to spend the day alone. I love how God takes care of me by putting people in my life when I need them. He's a pretty awesome God.

# APRIL 17, 2014

So, this evening, I gave my granddaughters their Bibles. I showed them how awesome they are and also gave them the journals and explained why I made them. I really hope they like them and use them and learn about Jesus and His love for them.

My youngest granddaughter came home with me to spend the weekend. When we got on the interstate, she got out her Bible and started reading Genesis. That just melted my heart! I explained that tomorrow we will be going to my church for something new that is being done this year, then we will go to the Passion Play. I was a little concerned about the intensity of the crucifixion, but I just knew she needed to see it. I wish other family members would see it, but some couldn't and some wouldn't. I can't make them, even though I really want to. My granddaughter read a little, and we talked about it for a little bit. I'm so excited for tomorrow!

# APRIL 18, 2014

Today was a super busy day, but so amazing. My granddaughter wanted scrambled eggs and pancakes for breakfast. That's hilarious cause I never cook breakfast or make pancakes. I eat eggs, but for supper, never breakfast. I tried to remember when I even made pancakes last. I'm pretty sure she was still sitting in a high chair! Seriously, that's the last time I ever made pancakes. That was 10 ½ years ago! So, I taught her how to make them. She had fun and they were yummy. She is also very creative and likes to sew. She made a couple of small pillows and we decided to make her mom a body pillow out of K-State fabric for Mother's Day. Then, we went to FBC for Journey To The Cross. It has seven interactive stations, with a book explaining the stations. Each station has a journey stop, response—look, think, listen, then prayer.

> Journey Stop #1 – The Garden of Gethsemane – Obedience – Matthew 26:38-43. The room was dark and quiet. It had a rock and a bench in a setting that really put you in the mood.

> Journey Stop #2 – The Garden/Outer Courtyard of the High Priest – Betrayal. Matthew 26:14-16 – Coins – Judas' Betrayal.

Journey Stop #3 – Arrest and Trial – accused. Matthew 26:55-56. In this room were some chains. The crowd was yelling to crucify Jesus and release Barabbas.

Journey Stop #4 – Punishment and Mockery – Suffered. Matthew 27:27-31. This room had the crown of thorns and the whip. I cringed when I felt those huge thorns. And to have it shoved on my head. Ouch! Then, there was the whip. I didn't know there were pieces of sharp bone and little balls of lead on the whip. I can't even imagine being beaten with this 39 times.

Journey Stop #5 – Confession – Transgression. Isaiah 53:4-6. The vinegar that Jesus was given when he said "I thirst". How horrible. There were white cards to write down our sins that were weighing us down.

Journey Stop #6 – The Cross – Sacrifice. Matthew 27:45-46, Matthew 27:50-51, 2 Corinthians 5:21. We were to take our sin card and a nail, and hammer our sin on the cross. Very powerful.

Journey Stop #7 – Communion – Forgiveness. Matthew 26:26-29. Hebrews 9:22 "Without the shedding of blood, there is no forgiveness of sins". Take communion—the bread for His body, the juice for the blood. Pray for people to know Jesus.

This was all very powerful, quiet, somber. It was an awesome beginning to our Easter weekend. For my granddaughter to have this up-close and personal experience, before going to the Passion Play, was extremely helpful. I pray this weekend opens her eyes to Jesus and helps her understand how much He loves her and how much she needs Him.

After a quick stop for something to eat and drink, we headed to the Passion Play. We got there at 5:15 p.m. The doors didn't open till 6:00 p.m., but there was already a line. She got a little bored and restless waiting for 45 minutes. She kept asking me what time is it? How many more minutes? Umm…only two minutes since you already asked me! We finally got inside and found a seat on the front row. Then, we had to wait an hour for it to start. My granddaughter was talking to the lady on the other side of her. Come to find out that this lady's sister is one of the nurses at my granddaughter's school! Small world.

The Passion started and my heart was so happy. My granddaughter was pretty much on the edge of her seat the whole time. She asked a few questions, and once in awhile she said she recognized a song or a verse. After the break was the arrest, trial, crucifixion, and resurrection of Jesus. Being on the front row, we had the cross dragged right beside us on the way up to the stage. We held hands during most of the rest. When Jesus was whipped, I reminded her of the bone and lead. That was so hard to watch. I reminded her about those long thorns on the crown. It was all very intense, but totally worth it. It was a packed house and was the last night of the play. I hope next year I can bring more family members and my other granddaughter. After the play, we talked about it and how much we liked it.

# Saturday, April 19, 2014

My church rents out TPAC—Topeka Performing Arts Center—every year for the Easter service. FBC does four services a weekend—two on Saturday evening and two on Sunday morning. Easter is a huge deal, so in order to have room for community members to join us, we have it at TPAC once on Saturday, once on Sunday. My friend and I were greeters, so my granddaughter helped greet. My in-laws, Ron's niece, husband and three kids came and saved us seats since greeters stay to greet till people stop coming in. Of course, the service was awesome, as always. My granddaughter had her new Bible and I taught her to underline the verses that Pastor was reading. Buckets were passed out with response cards to fill out. There were several questions for people to mark the appropriate box. I don't remember the exact words or number of boxes. The first box said something like "I believed for the first time". Another box was about being reconnected again; another box was about wanting prayer for sharing the Gospel with others and to list the first names of people you want to share with. I don't remember the other boxes. I marked prayers for others I wanted to share with. I noticed my granddaughter marked the first box! I was happy and also unsure if she was aware of what she did. I got to thinking maybe she thought she had to mark a box, so she just marked one. After that, the cards were collected in buckets with the offering, and the service continued with worship music. Awesome! The pastor said if people needed prayer or if they marked the first box to go to them after the service. I took my granddaughter down to talk to him. I was excited, yet wondered what she would say about checking that first box. Pastor asked her about it. I don't remember her exact words, but she said something like she had been listening to what people had been saying about what all Jesus had done for her, and that she should believe in Him and trust Him. So, she decided she should do that. I had to smile and almost cried happy tears! My pastor told her she made his Easter. He prayed and we left. When we got home, she asked some questions like why was Good Friday called "Good" when that's the day Jesus was crucified? We talked about it for a little while. We talked at supper about things in her life she has suffered through, but how God helped her through it. How He answered her prayers. How sometimes God allows us to suffer, how we don't always understand why, and about God's timing and our wanting things to happen in our time. How God knows way more than we do and sees the whole picture and we can't. How he knows what's best for us—even when we think we have all the answers and have it all figured out. She is so smart and she gets this God thing. I have a feeling God is going to use her in a big way somehow, some way. I am one tired and happy grandma! It's been a crazy busy weekend, but also full of amazing things that God has done in just a couple of days. It was good to have some time…just us, bonding, laughing, eating, and learning. I love her so very much.

# Easter Sunday, April 20, 2014

Had to take granddaughter back home—boo! Ron's mom called me in the afternoon. Her voice sounded like she had been crying. I was afraid something was wrong. She said she loved the second spiral notebook I gave them to read. She said she loved it and me and was glad all the glory is going to God. It has to—these aren't my words. We talked about different parts of it and how God used Ron for all of this to happen. I told her I still didn't think it was fair—God could have used Ron and let him stay here. God uses people all the time without taking spouses or loved ones away. I don't understand or like this whole thing, but it's God's plan, not ours. I went to their house for awhile to visit with them, Ron's niece, husband, three kids, and Ron's niece's significant other. Was good to see them all. I am so very blessed.

So, now, its 11:20 p.m. on Easter night. My plan was to go to bed early to recuperate from an amazing, fun, and busy weekend with my granddaughter and then this afternoon with Ron's mom and dad, niece, husband and kids, another niece and fiance'. I have to get up early in the morning and, remember, I am NOT a morning person! As I'm ready for bed, I'm being led to write this. Really, God? You know how tired I am! And this is so personal. I don't want to write this. But, I have to, so here goes…

Last night, someone I love texted me and asked for something from Sonic. This person almost always gets McDonald's. Since this person doesnt drive, I help get food. On my way home from delivering the food, I got a text saying I messed up the order. The drink wasn't the largest one. The tots didn:t have cheese, which I don:t remember hearing Anyways, the order was messed up. so, instead of being thankful for food at all, I get a text saying it:s trash. More hateful texts followed, which I ignored. But, also what it means to me is that isn't this what we tell God? Don't we tell Him to "stay far, far away from me"? Sometimes, we yell at God. We reject Him. We swear at Him. We tell Him that He messed up our prayer order—like a Sonic order—I want this and this, without this and that. Make this a Route 44—the biggest there is. Oh, yeah, add cheese to make it more yummy. We get mad when God gives us something else than what we ordered. Didn't God know we wanted the biggest? The cheese? He knows our thoughts before we do, so why did He mess it up? So, when He doesn't give us what we ask for, don't we get mad and tell to "stay far, far away', "I'll starve", that He gave us "trash"? Don't we tell Him we don't need His Word, His guidance— that spiritual milk? We think we can do just fine without him. Don't you think God is heartbroken over our decisions? Our rejection? Our ignorance? He sees what we need and we refuse it. Then, we wonder why we are so miserable. We think we know it all—news flash! We don't. We're human; He's God. There's no competition.

Imagine how God feels over all of us? Remember, Jesus wept. He's waiting for us to ask Him for help. He knows what we need. We have to ask and trust. He's on the other side of the door, waiting for us to invite Him in. There is not a doorknob on the other side of the door. We have to open it and invite Him in. He's there, waiting. Keep on asking, and you will be given what you ask for. Keep on looking, and you will find. Keep on knocking, and the door will be opened for everyone who asks, receives. Everyone who seeks, finds. And the door is opened to everyone who knocks" (Matthew 7:7-8).

# APRIL 24, 2014

Sometimes, I don't feel God tugging at me for awhile. Then, there are times when He just doesn't stop.

At Ron's mom and dad's house on Easter, they were telling us stories about different trips they have been on. Most were trips away from the U.S. I love hearing them talk about their trips. I asked if they have ever been to the Holy Land before. I don't have a clue where that came from! I sure didn't think about it. It just blurted out. Ever since then, I feel a tug to go there. Don't ask me where that came from cause I never really thought about going there. It's expensive. I'm stressing over going a couple hours away to Excelsior Springs! I love the mountains. I would love to go to see my niece and family in Alaska. I have always wanted to go see Idaho, Montana, Wyoming—the pretty part—South Dakota, Canada, more of Colorado, anyplace west, north, and beautiful.

One reason, besides expense, I never thought of going out of the U.S. is that I'm terrified of water! Guess what? To get to the Holy Land, you gotta fly across the ocean! That's a lot of WATER!!

But, after seeing the Passion Play and all the Easter activities, I really feel tugged to go there. To walk where Jesus walked. How amazing will that be? I also feel like I'm being told to write about it. As in another book. A book about walking where Jesus walked and telling everyone about it. All the places. How it feels to be there. And talk about beautiful! So, another leap of faith—I don't have a clue how I can afford it. And I know I will not do this trip alone. I need a photographer. You can't possibly go to the Holy Land without a photographer. I don't have a camera, except for my phone. But...I know who does!

I didn't think there would be another book. This is about Ron and God and whenever this is done, I figured the book writing would be done, too. Guess not. What an honor to be led to go to the Holy Land and write about it! Somehow, some way, God will work out the details. He's God. He's good at things like this. I just have to be patient and sometimes I'm not so good at that! I have to trust, believe, and obey. I have absolutely no idea when or how this trip can happen. Not a clue. I'm pretty excited, though. Except for the flying across the ocean part. That scares the bejeebers out of me! God really has a sense of humor, watching me sweat that part!

I think a lot about the inscription on our grave stone—walking with Jesus. It takes my breath away when I think that Ron is walking with Jesus. That's the ultimate experience. Nothing on this Earth can top that! But, the thought of walking where Jesus walked here on Earth just blows my mind. I think that's got to be the ultimate experience here on Earth. The more I let myself think about it, the more excited I get. Am I there yet?!

# May 13, 2014

Friday, May 2nd, I took Willow to be spayed. It's hard to believe she's 6 months old already. It was so hard to leave her. I had her boarded till Monday, the 6th. My granddaughter and I had a busy weekend planned, so I left her there. When I picked her up, I was told to keep her calm and quiet for 7-10 days. Great. She's a 6-month-old Lab puppy! And she lives with a Westie and a cat she loves to romp with and chase. I have 14 steps upstairs where we all sleep and where I kennel her. Keeping them all separated is going to be a trip. I was concerned about her going up and down the steps so much. So, I drug her huge kennel downstairs to my tiny living room. Nighttime was the hardest. I'm used to her sleeping in her kennel in my room. She doesn't get to sleep on the bed yet, since she's still in the chewing stage. She would have a blast, chewing whatever she wanted and I would sleep right through it! She's pretty much potty trained, but I don't trust her all night, unsupervised. Since I'm a good puppy mommy, I hated the thought of her sleeping in the living room alone. So, I slept on the loveseat with Lucky, who hogs whatever space she can. She is a diva dog and likes to be comfy. Let's just say I didn't sleep very well. I'm short, but my loveseat is shorter! I tossed and turned, and disrupted Lucky in the process. The kennel was right beside me. One thing about fibro is that not sleeping well makes the pain worse. I told myself I wasn't going to do that again. Until Tuesday night. I just felt guilty sleeping in my comfy bed and her downstairs in her kennel alone. So, I slept on the loveseat again, and Wednesday and Thursday. Friday, I had to sleep in a bed! Willow is loud enough to wake me up when she needs out in the mornings. During the days, she misses playing with Lucky. Lucky is enjoying Willow being in her kennel when Lucky gets her turn being out with me. Lucky sure seems to know how to push Willow's buttons. She will get a toy—one they usually wrestle over--and lay right where Willow can see her. Willow usually voices her annoyance with this by whining or barking a little. Lucky waits till Willow stops, then walks right in front of the kennel and sits in front of the door. That's so cruel! It's like "ha, ha—you can't get me!" These dogs are such good therapy and company. They make me laugh. When it's Willow's turn to be out with me, Lucky gets to stay in the bedroom upstairs. Willow plays with her toys. When she gets tired, she crawls up in my chair with me. When she sits up beside me, she is taller than me now. She lays her chin on my shoulder and puts her paw on my arm like she's giving me a side hug. Or, she puts her nose behind my neck. She melts my heart. When she's tired, she comes to momma. She doesn't seem to care if I'm doing my journaling, reading the Bible, or writing anything. She loves to cuddle. She's 42 pounds now. I know she's going to get a lot bigger. Good thing this chair of Ron's is wide!

One thing I love about my animals—all animals--is that they don't hold grudges. They don't hate, they forgive. No matter how bad of a day I may have, they understand. They just love unconditionally. Just like Jesus. He forgives us. He is always there to love us, no matter what. Sometimes, I don't feel worthy of my animals' awesomeness, their unconditional love. Sometimes, I don't feel worthy of God's unconditional love. It's sure nice to know my Willow and Lucky, and Ron's cat, Savannah, are always there for me. They give me way more than I give them. No amount of treats or toys can repay them for their love. Just like there is no way—ever—we can repay God for His love. For Jesus dying on the cross for you, for me, for all of us. We don't deserve His love, but He gives it to us unconditionally. Just like my animals. I'm so glad God made them. I'm so thankful He is trusting me to be their doggy mommy and kitty mommy. It's hard work, especially now, having to keep an active, crazy, wild 6-month-old puppy calm and separated from the others. It's not like I have a huge place and lots of options for them. But, the time is almost up and it was good to have separate bonding time. Just like I need my quiet time alone with God. In the mornings, throughout the day, and at night. And, I never forget to thank Him for my animals and their unconditional love. And God, for His. I cannot imagine my life without these animals. Especially after Ron passed. Sometimes, when they are sleeping, I just hug them and don't want to let go. My life is happier, peaceful, and full of love with my animals. Just like my life is happier, peaceful, and full of love with God. I remember when Willow was 6 weeks old. I could hold her in the palm of my hand. She's outgrown my palm. God holds us in His hand and we cannot ever outgrow His hand. That's very comforting to me.

May 6th was Ron's mom's birthday. I got the honor of going to lunch with his mom and dad. It's always so good to spend time with them. We laugh, we talk, and of course, we eat. It's so hard to see the empty seat beside me. I cannot imagine how hard it is for them, especially on her birthday, to not have Ron here at lunch with us. Or no phone call from their only daughter, who passed away a couple of years before Ron did. I know it's hard on my birthday to not have my parents and Ron here. I cannot imagine my birthday with my only daughter and baby boy both in Heaven. But, they both have faith. They both know they will see them again someday, and cannot wait. I can't wait to get to heaven either. Our tiny brains cannot begin to imagine how incredibly awesome it's going to be! But, until we get to see Ron, his sister, my parents, nephew, brother-in-law, aunts, uncles, and grandparents, we will enjoy being together here in this broken, messed-up world. The empty seat is still painful, but I know it's necessary to continue going on and telling this story. A story where I'm the luckiest girl on the planet cause God blessed me with Ron and his mom and dad. I really don't understand God's timing cause I really coulda used having these relationships years ago. Maybe He thought if I had to wait, I would appreciate them more, and I do. I miss some of the people in my life in Manhattan and before Ron. I will never forget them, the happy times and the sad times. Those times were necessary, too—good and bad. They are all part of this story. This journey that I am now on.

Sometimes, I don't feel worthy to be a part of such an awesome family. I have been blessed so much. I kinda feel like they lost Ron and are stuck with me. Sometimes, I feel guilty cause I'm here and Ron isn't. But, then I feel like Ron is the one who got the best deal out of all of us. He's walking with Jesus!

After a great lunch with them, the next day wasn't so great. On May 7th, Ron's dad had a stroke. I'm not giving the details and he's OK. Thank God! And God was totally taking care of him. He was on our church's emergency prayer chain. Both of our small groups were praying. They had many friends and family praying. I posted my request I always post on Facebook, asking to please pray—God knows who for and why. I don't give details. Within minutes, I had many friends and family asking what was going on. I privately messaged them. Just amazed that besides my Topeka friends and my family in the Manhattan and Wamego areas, I had friends and family praying for him in Alaska, Iowa, Missouri, Oklahoma, Texas, Nevada, western Kansas, and other parts of Kansas. I'm probably leaving out someplace and if I did and you are reading this, I am sorry. That's just my friends and family. My friends told their friends or their church prayer warriors. God heard those prayers and answered them. After a night in ICU and several days in a regular room, he is home. I continue to pray for him. He is an amazing man and I'm not ready for God to take him away from me. Or Ron's mom. They've known each other forever. You know, he's the football player; she's the cheerleader. He's homecoming king; she's homecoming queen. Married right after high school and still together. What a legacy, a godly legacy, about how it's supposed to be done and done right. So, this time, I am happy with God's timing to let us keep him here and without any major problems from the stroke.

# May 13, 2014

Memory Book. Anyone ever do a memory book? It's a scrapbook about a loved one who has passed away. My grief counselor told me about this group when I started the widows group. So, it's been awhile and I had intentions of going. Intentions don't really mean anything, though. I have a procrastination problem. I love to take pictures. A zillion pics. My problem is getting the physical pictures. It's kinda hard to make a scrapbook about my life with Ron without physical pictures. I have a bunch on CDs that need printed. It's not hard...I just gotta do it. I still have a lot on my computer that isn't working. Some way, somehow, I need to get those pictures.

Yesterday, I finally stopped in this little scrapbooking store that I drive by all the time. I always tell myself I need to go in there. I'm always either in a hurry, broke, just not in the mood, or it's after hours. Looking around yesterday got me inspired. I saw things that I have not seen in other places. I didn't buy anything, but I got ideas. Then, last night, I remembered I had coupons from JoAnn's that were about to expire. I zoomed there to look at the scrapbooks and paper. I was told the memory group supplies books, paper, and has the fancy gadgets to make everything look good and whatever else is needed. I wanted to pick out my own book, though, and some paper. I got a scrapbook for half price, a pad of wedding paper—yeah, that's gonna be rough! I found a pad of Live by Faith paper. I forgot my coupons, but there was one in the store. I got the book and wedding paper. Then, today, I took my coupon and went and got half off the Live by Faith paper.

I have never seen paper like this. It's pretty awesome. I went back to the scrapbook shop and bought individual pages. A wedding one, and some other pages—they even make State ones! Got a couple of different State ones, one that even says Topeka, Capital City of Kansas! Saw some Chiefs stuff—no Broncos or Green Bay—that's messed up, but Ron loved the Chiefs, so that worked. Then, I about cried. I saw some "In memory of" paper and "In loving memory" rub-ons. Ouch! Wasn't expecting that. Picking out the pages was hard enough because each page is for a special memory. I was so afraid the lady checking me out was going to comment on them, or ask questions. I didn't want to have to cry. So, I have a book. I have some special paper. Now, I just have to get in gear and get some pictures printed. I have six days left till group. I have to make myself do this. Pictures are hard. It's gonna slap me in the face when I see them on whatever that machine is called in Wal-Mart. I don't want to cry in Wal-Mart either. But, I have to do it. I can't go to Memory Group without pictures. Wish me luck--I'm sure going to need it!

Oh, yeah, one of the individual pages is a blue sky with clouds. It's called "October Afternoon". I couldn't believe it when I saw it. We disconnected Ron from life support on October 2nd. My father passed away in October, too. Who would have thought that pages would be so heartbreaking? Gut wrenching? Whoever makes them sure knows how to play on emotions. It works.

## May 14, 2014

I got brave and went to print pics for Tuesday's Memory Book Group. We don't have pics of us until the wedding. So, I have 39 wedding pics. It wasn't hard, like I thought it would be. I was really concerned about breaking down in Wal-Mart, while selecting the pics. But, I didn't. The kid who had to teach me how to use the machine was very nice. I got in and out pretty fast like. I decided to put the pics in order and look through this wicker picnic basket I have my wedding and honeymoon pictures in. I found a little paper from The Elms that had our room number on it. When I called to reserve a room awhile back, I asked if they could look up the room. For some reason, they don't have info. that far back? Really? Seven years isn't that long! I was also told the hotel had done major remodeling, so the room wouldn't look the same anyway. Doesn't matter. If I am going to do this, I want the same room. I called the hotel to see if the room we had was available. It wasn't reserved, so I will be staying in the same room. I am actually getting a little excited about going. I'm not really sure why I have to do this now, but I will obey and go. This will be the only trip I have ever been on alone the whole time. No one on the other end when I get there. It's not that far from here. It's just that it's something I have not done before. I am trying to not have expectations. Except, I do expect to smile, cry, and write. Whatever else happens will happen. Oh, yeah, I'll have to take pictures and hit the places we ate at and a few small shops. That's what I expect. So, we shall see what happens when I get there!

# MAY 15, 2014

Today, I met with my grief counselor. I told him I finally got in gear and got pictures printed and bought scrapbook stuff. Well, guess what? I procrastinated so long that the group has fizzled out. Great! I am totally kicking myself for dragging my heels. I'm finally ready. It's like being all dressed up and no place to go. I have the stuff, but no group to go to. Grrr…It will start up in the Fall—September through November—then again in the Spring. I'm so sad. I'm so mad at myself. I was scared and I let that fear run over me. He suggested I spend this time laying out my pages and putting together paper, pics and words I want to write in the sleeve for each page. That way, when the group starts, everything will be ready and I can just put it all together and it should go pretty quick. So, all the drama, all the dragging my heels, has made me have to do this on my own till September.

# MAY 25, 2014

I got my baby fix for the month in the nursery at church this morning. I just love those babies! I do get sad, though, when they grow up and graduate to the one-year-old room.

After that, I went to the cemetery. My friend makes duct tape flowers on dowel rods that fit in the vases on the stone. I bought two that were different red, white, and blue ones. I found a small flag-shaped mylar balloon. I took them all to trade out the other duct tape flowers I put there about a year ago. Those were Chiefs colors. There were some yellow flowers there. Ron's mom and dad beat me there! They look so nice and fresh. The cemetery looked all freshened up for Memorial Day weekend. Today is Sunday, so I'm sure it will look even better tomorrow.

Was kind of a slow, quiet day today. Lots of things I should have done, but no energy. Mostly spent time with my dogs. I truly would be lost without them, especially on days like today. This evening, I decided I should get out the scrapbook paper and start laying out the pages. The only pics I have printed now are the 39 wedding pictures. It didn't take me long to pick out paper and pics for each page. My problem was that when I was done, I only had two pages left in my book! Geeze, that was just our wedding. How am I going to get four years of pictures into one book? So, I called my friend who scrapbooks. She told me to pick a few pictures from each event. A few? Seriously? Really? How do I pick a few pictures from our wedding? It was very small, but those 39 pictures are all important to me. How do I not include them? She also said I can add pages to my book. So, I grabbed my awesome JoAnn's coupons and went to buy more pages. Figures. I'm always late. I forgot JoAnn's closes early on Sundays. So, I went to Wally World. Of course, they didn't have the pages I needed. I got some templates to use to cut my pics. I don't have all the fancy scrapbook stuff. I have done a couple of books and they came out just fine. But, this is Ron's memory book. It has to be better than fine. It has to be amazing. Somehow…

# May 26, 2014

Very long quiet day. Decided to get more scrapbook pages for memory book. Spent most of today, Memorial Day, working on picking out paper, pics, cutting pics, and putting in page protectors. Got wedding and honeymoon pages laid out. Took a break and went to the cemetery. The mylar flag balloon I put there yesterday was gone. The flowers that Ron's mom and dad put there and the flowers on dowel rods were still there. The balloon was on a stick, in between the dowel rod flowers. The vase has rubbery stuff to grip things. The wind wasn't blowing, for once. I have a feeling someone stole it. Makes me sad. I didn't stay long. Too many people around. When I was leaving the cemetery, I saw a young lady sitting on the ground by a heavily decorated grave. She was all alone. I wondered if she was a widow, too, or if it was the grave of her parents, a sibling, another family member, or a very good friend. I just prayed for her when I drove by. I remember sitting at Ron's grave. Sometimes, I would talk to him. I would remember the tent, the wind, the people, the pastor, the love, and the tears that day. Today, I was mostly alone, but it was OK. I had my animals, saw my son for a few minutes, talked to my neighbor a few times, but mainly focused on Ron and the memories. I really miss my mom and dad, too. And my grandparents, brother-in-law, aunts and uncles, and also thinking of my nephew who passed away last month. Praying for the daughter he left behind. I know all these people are in Heaven and I will see them again someday, in their new bodies--not old or sick, not sad, not lonely. But, they are happy and walking with Jesus. It's just so hard for us on this Earth. Us left behind in this crazy, messed-up, broken world, trying to make sense of stuff that doesn't make sense and won't make sense till we are in Heaven and see the whole picture. Until then, all we have are the memories in our head, or the ones we capture and make into memory books to remember those good times, fun times, family, friends, pets. Those books can be passed down to other loved ones and other generations to come. But, maybe it's a better idea to make the scrapbooks while our loved ones are still alive, so the pictures don't hurt so much. But, then again, I believe that as hard as it is to look at them, this is what needs to be done for healing in this part of my grief journey. Maybe it was needed now, before I go to Excelsior Springs on what would have been our seventh wedding anniversary, on July 7th. I wonder how many more pictures, memories, tears will happen before then? I don't have a clue, but God knows and He will get me through it.

# June 6, 2014

Haven't had time to write for awhile. Monday at widows group we were given two pieces of paper. Our topic was guilt. The first paper is called Reconciliation of a Penitent. It's about confessions and forgiveness. It's about writing a letter to our spouses, asking forgiveness for whatever it may be. About confessing whatever is on our hearts. All the woulda's, coulda's, shoulda's, if only's, what if's, and so on. All that baggage we carry around, weighing us down. It's not healthy. Most of us know it, but do it anyway. We are usually our own best enemies, beating ourselves up. There is rational guilt and irrational guilt. We are experts at telling ourselves we are guilty of this or that. In reality, we probably aren't. If we are guilty of something, we probably blow it way out of proportion. Then again, some people blame and refuse to accept any responsibility for anything. That's an extreme—the opposite direction. Telling ourselves not to feel guilty doesn't work. We need to write a letter to our spouse, or anyone really, confessing whatever it may be and then asking for forgiveness. Our grief counselor stated, "Confession needs to be as messy as the sin."

The second sheet is blank, except at the top it says A Letter Asking Your Forgiveness. The back says A Letter From You That Forgives Me. That's a letter saying what we think our loved one would say in response to my letter asking forgiveness. Will we be forgiven? Maybe the sin really is bad and our loved one will not forgive us. Maybe we need to write several letters back and forth. I have not had time to sit down and write it yet, but I will. Writing is very therapeutic for me. I won't write the letter or specifics here, but I'm sure I will have something to say about the process and emotions involved in writing my letter and the one I write from him to me.

Something else that has consumed my thoughts this week is LaVeta, Colorado. Ever been there? It's a tiny, sleepy town of around 800 or 900 people, an hour southwest of Pueblo, Colorado. It's at the base of the Spanish Peaks. I know this has to be a God thing. Here's the story of LaVeta, Colorado. The more I think about it, the more awe I feel, and excited, and hopeful, and lots of other things—all positive.

Last summer, my friend since third grade, and I finally made our trip to Colorado. We lost touch 32 years ago and I finally found her in November 2012 on Facebook. Our dream was to go to Colorado after high school in Colby, Kansas. Well, life happened and we each went in different directions. Anyway, we lost touch, found each other, and made promises to get to Colorado. I searched and found us a cabin from a Saturday to a Monday, last summer. We wanted a place to stay on the Friday before. I Googled places close to the cabin, but wasn't having any luck. I found LaVeta. I called B&Bs, but there was a family reunion in town and they were all booked up. A lady asked if I called "I Love Lucy RV Park". Really? I laughed and told her it didn't come up when I was asking Google where to stay in LaVeta. I told her I didn't have an RV or camper. She said there are two retro Airstreams. One is named Lucy; one is Ricky. I called the RV park and explained that we only could stay one night—they had a two-night minimum. She called me back the next day and said we could stay in Ricky for one night. My friend and I laughed and laughed—said God really had a sense of humor, throwing this adventure in our trip. Seemed like forever before the night finally came for me to leave on the Amtrak for Garden City, where she was going to meet me at 6-something AM. Ron's mom and dad took me to the train station. I never rode the train before, so it was a new adventure. I was excited and nervous. People told me the Amtrak rocks you to sleep. NOT ME! It was around midnight when I got on. I had no clue where to go. I was told in a hurry, since there were people behind me. Oh, yeah, I learned not to pack so much that my duffle bag didn't break my arm trying to carry it through an aisle with sleeping people's arms, legs, pillows, and blankets hanging over the arm rests. That was an adventure right there and not a fun one! It was dark, except for tiny night lights. I wasn't in my seat before the train started moving again. It made it harder to try and walk without falling on people or bumping into them. I am a klutz and not a world traveler, so this definitely was an experience! Of course, my seat was by the window, so I had to crawl over the person on the aisle seat. Oh, yeah, trying to put my suitcase above the seat while the train was moving was kinda hard, too, cause I'm so short! So, I finally got settled in my seat. The other person went back to sleep after telling me she was going to southern California. Geeze, I was ready to get off then because of how rocky it was! Can't imagine riding that far. I couldn't sleep. The train was clickety-clacking and it seemed like we were tipping at times and it was dark, so people didn't want to talk to me. Before the girl beside me went back to sleep, she told me about the car with the windows, so I could see out and hang out there if I couldn't sleep. So, after discovering I had NO CELL SERVICE after about Emporia, I was not a happy camper. No Facebook, couldn't ask Google any questions, couldn't post my status of leaving Kansas or being on a bumpy train. So, I climbed over her—or at least I felt like it's what I did. Of course, she was tall and had long legs all stretched out. That was fun, trying not to fall on my face or the person across the aisle sleeping! I found the car with the windows—there were a few people in there; some were sleeping. No one was talking there either. I know it was late, but I seriously was wide awake and ready to talk to people. Again, like I was all dressed up and no place to go. It was kinda cool, going through tiny towns with everything dark. I wondered about the people living there, out in the middle of nowhere, in south central Kansas. One thing I realized was that there are no signs saying the names of the towns. Never had a reason to know that they don't put those signs by the train tracks! I wondered if the people were happy, sad, lonely, in love, divorced, widowed, had kids, lost a loved one, in debt, debt-free, worried, or at peace. I always wonder about things like this when I see jets in the sky. Are people going to someplace? Are they running away from someone or someplace? Happy? Hurt? Do you ever wonder these things? I have, since I was a kid, lying on the grass, watching the jets zoom by. Always wondered where they were going.

I stayed in the window car, or whatever it's called. It was last year, so I don't remember and I'm too lazy to ask Google right now. The staff came by and informed me I had to be in my seat or down where I got off when my stop came. If I fell asleep and am not in my seat, they don't know where to find me to tell me to get off. It seemed like eternity, but the sun started to come up. It was beautiful. I rarely see sunrises, so I thanked God for giving me a beautiful sunrise that morning. I got off, found my friend, and we were off to Colorado! It was supposed to only be about four hours to LaVeta. We stopped a lot for pit stops, so it was longer. We had a blast, talking and catching up. We laughed a lot and got lost a couple of times, but that was all part of the adventure. When we got to the Colorado border, she wrote on the sign about how we finally made it! We took pics of the sign, her message, and her by the sign. I still didn't have any signal, so couldn't post anything on Facebook! How irritating, not to be able to share such an important time—finally getting to Colorado with my friend after all these years! The world—well at least my Facebook world—needed to know this! We made it closer to the mountains. We were super excited when we could start to see the front range. The outline of blue mountains. They were still tiny, but it was really happening! I'm writing this a year later and my heart is beating super-fast, just picturing that first glimpse of the mountains. I'm not a world traveler, but I dearly love the mountains. Growing up in Colby, we went to Denver and Colorado Springs a lot. My paternal grandma, two aunts, and three uncles lived there. I remember my grandma's beautiful flower garden. I remember the zoo, some huge dinosaur museum, Elitches, and Cinderella City mall. I remember running up and down the steps at Red Rocks. I never made it back to a concert, but I will! I also remember the airplanes landing or taking off over the top of the road--we went under it. I can still hear that noise and hoping those planes didn't land on us by breaking the road! That was the old airport. I also remember the ice cream truck clanging its bell at my grandma's street and running to catch it. I also remember, for some insane reason, my parents taking me to a drug store by my grandma's house and buying me a couple of goldfish in a baggie, to hold all the way back to Colby. They rarely made it. Usually, they ended up floating to the top of the water, staring at me with their eyes on the sides of their heads. I can still see those dead goldfish in the baggie. It made me mad cause they died. I was mad cause I really didn't like fish when they were alive. I really didn't like them floating and staring at me. I still hate fish. They have weird eyes. And their gills are pretty bizarre, too. So, lots of memories as a kid in Denver. Oh, yeah, and my mom and dad putting my school clothes on layaway in Denver or Colorado Springs. Colby didn't have many places to shop. Wal-Mart hadn't invaded everyplace yet. My clothes were from places I can't remember, but I do remember the malls. The only place, besides Colorado and a few places in Colby, to shop was McCook, Nebraska. We didn't go there much. Colorado was way cooler. I don't know if cooler is a word like that, but I just made it one. My two brothers and my sister all lived in Colorado Springs. Since there is a nine years difference between myself and my next sibling, I was like an only child. He left for Colorado Springs soon after high school. I fell in love with Colorado Springs. I loved it more than Denver. My grandma in Denver passed away when I was in third grade. I remember it was third grade because my favorite teacher was reading Charlotte's Web and I had to miss it for my grandma's funeral. So, we really didn't go to Denver much after that. I remember that after Limon, Colorado, I could eventually see the outline of Pike's Peak and the front range. Wow, my heart just started beating fast, writing about those moments I was sticking my head between my mom and dad's seats, anxiously waiting to see the tiniest glimpses of the front range. We didn't have seat belts then, so I always sat as close to the front as I could. I remember asking my mom and dad over and over why I couldn't see people skiing down the mountains. We never skied. Good thing...I'm a klutz. But, as we got closer and closer to the mountains, I just couldn't understand why, if all these people were in Colorado skiing, I couldn't see them. I don't remember what they told me. I wonder if they dreaded the moment from when I saw the mountains to all the way there—me asking questions.

I loved Garden of The Gods, Seven Falls, and Broadmoore, where the people trained for Olympic skating. I loved Manitou Springs. I loved the little hippie shops. I always wanted a little shop. I wanted to make pottery and have a pottery shop. We always stayed in these little cabins in Cascade, just west of Manitou Springs. I was the happiest ever when we were in Colorado, especially in the mountains. Before my brother moved there, when we went there on vacations, I remember the cabin being one huge room with three beds and a bathroom. The kitchenette was awesome because one of my best memories ever was waking up to the smells of my mom cooking bacon, eggs, pancakes, or French toast and the smell of the coffee brewing. I can still smell those smells. I remember my brother teaching me how to hike the hills behind the cabin. You always walk down sideways. Trust me, it works cause walking down front-ways only makes you slide and fall. I can still smell that mountain air. The pine trees were amazing. I drove my parents crazy, collecting pine cones and rocks to take back to Colby. Sometimes, I would find little pieces of driftwood. Across from the cabins was Santa's Workshop. We never went there, but I remember watching the Ferris wheel go round and round. I wish those cabins were still there. Those were truly my favorite childhood memories. I loved the drives through the mountains. I don't have a clue where we went, but it was beautiful. We had a few picnics in the mountains. I remember some scary, dark, and noisy tunnels! I can still see this beautiful, amazing double rainbow when we came out of a tunnel. I also remember my brother scaring me by telling me stories about the tunnels being haunted because of the people who died working on the bridges and tunnels. I remember Glenwood Springs. It stunk! It smelled like sulfur. I hated it. I remember donkeys walking around the streets of Cripple Creek. I remember being scared to death, walking on the bridge at Royal Gorge. My mom and I walked along the side; my dad drove beside us. That doesn't make sense to me now. Why would they let cars and pedestrians on a road crossing that high? I remember many things about Colorado. I remember the thing that always broke my heart was having to leave. I remember being in the back seat, looking out the back window, watching the front range get smaller and smaller. I remember crying almost every time. I felt I belonged there.

I hated leaving my brothers or my sister and the mountains. I believed it was God's Country. It had to be. There was no way it could not be a God thing. No way. I remember one time before we left Colorado Springs, we went up someplace and looked down over the city. It was at night and it was beautiful. This was ages ago—in the sixties and early seventies. I cannot imagine what it looks like now. That night, we left at dark. I looked out the back window as long as I could—just looking at how magical all those lights looked, twinkling just like the stars I saw above them twinkling. I will never forget that night or those amazing memories. I remember as a teenager listening to John Denver. I even had those dorky glasses I got from a little shop in Manitou. I thought those were pretty cool! John Denver sang how I felt. I never got to go to Aspen, where he lived. I can only imagine that beauty! I remember having a dream in high school—living in Wamego, Kansas—that I was looking down on my funeral. I was all about blue jeans, t-shirt, and barefoot--or moccasins. I always told my parents and family I wanted to be buried in my blue jeans, t-shirt, and barefoot. In my dream, my funeral was outside in the mountains. People were sitting in a circle and John Denver was singing at my funeral. I remember seeing myself in my casket in jeans, t-shirt, and bare footed, just like I asked. I don't remember a lot of dreams, especially from 1976, but I remember that dream and house we lived in then.

Boy, did I get off on a very long bunny trail! I guess I needed to explain my love for the mountains and how excited those first glimpses of them make me.

So, when my friend and I saw those mountains, they were not of the ones in Denver, or the ones of Pike's Peak and Manitou Mountain. They were a range I had not seen in years, and I really did not remember much about them except the Twin Peaks. I only remember seeing them from the highway from Pueblo to Trinidad when I was in junior high.

As we drove closer and the mountains got bigger to us, something happened inside. We stopped in Walsenburg for a pit stop, gas, and to stretch. I remember that drive around the bend and the peaks were amazing. Then, we saw the tiny dots at the bottom that was LaVeta. At first, I was disappointed. I was hoping it was in the mountains more.

We turned off and headed into LaVeta. We found "I Love Lucy RV Park". Part of me knew this place, and this tiny town was special. But, I had no clue how that trip has made my mind go crazy one year later.

We checked in and unloaded only what we needed for the rest of the evening and morning. We found a Mexican place to eat. We went back and took a little nap. She had been up super early to drive two hours to get me in Garden City, and I had not slept on the train or the day before. We got up and went to a neat little place for supper. There was an ice cream social for people in the RV Park, so we went back for that. We were a little late getting back. There is a tiny stage by the office where someone either from LaVeta, or someone staying in the park, was singing. Everyone had their chairs sitting around the stage. It started to pour, so we crowded inside the office, with the ice cream, of course! It is a small, but very cozy, office. Pictures of Lucy all over. A pot-belly stove that was going, a small table that now had ice cream on it. My friend had made some cookies and brought them along. She gave people some. Of course, they were amazing! People were visiting, asking us where we were from. Seems like the others knew each other. So, we told our story about how we were friends since third grade, I moved away when I was 16, and we stayed in touch till our oldest kids were two and three. Now, we are grandmas! The owners of Lucy and the other people staying in the park were so very friendly. It was pouring outside. That rain smelled so good. It was dark and that good old mountain-fresh air just flooded my brain. I knew standing in that office that these were special people, and LaVeta was a special place. People slowly went back to their RVs or campers. We went to the Ricky Airstream. We had to laugh at how retro it was. How old, but cute. The beds were about a foot and a half apart, if that much. The sliding door to the tiny bathroom was at our heads. It was very small, but I loved it. God did have a sense of humor. I Love Lucy RV Park in LaVeta, Colorado! On Saturday, we woke up and ate some monkey bread my friend had made. The owner and a friend of hers told us about a farmer's market downtown. By the way, LaVeta has two streets that are paved! The others are dirt or gravel—I don't remember. I do remember walking on the street to the corner end of the RV park. There were the Spanish Peaks, just as beautiful as could be. And huge! Not tiny images. It was a beautiful, sunny Colorado morning and that good old mountain air and looking at those peaks got me. I knew, standing there, that I belonged here. In LaVeta, Colorado. A tiny town with a great view of the Spanish Peaks. The owner also told us of an art show in Cuchara, a few miles southwest. So, we went exploring downtown LaVeta first. I fell in love with the few little shops on Main Street. Everyone was so friendly. And that air! Did I mention I love that fresh mountain air?! I can smell it right now. I miss it terribly. The shop owners know tourists when they see them. They asked us where we lived, so we told them our story, too. We had a blast, walking around on Main Street—all two or three blocks of it! We drove around town a little. It was so cool to see deer walking around in the yards. I imagine the people didn't appreciate the deer munching on their plants. The deer just looked at us like asking us what are we looking at? Well, living in Topeka, Kansas, I don't see deer wandering the streets or in people's yards—that's what I was looking at!

We decided to go to Cuchara and check out the art fair. We had awhile before we could get in our cabin. The short drive to Cuchara was gorgeous. Around every bend was a new spectacular view. We went to the art show—saw some very beautiful work by very talented artists. Then, we ate at this cool place that had a big outdoor patio. They got slammed with customers all at once, so we had to wait awhile for our food. It was OK. More time to talk, laugh, dream, and dream some more. The view from the place was just beautiful. I could easily go there for lunch every single day for the rest of my life and never get tired of the view. Never. We left Cuchara and drove back through LaVeta to the highway to go west to find our cabin. I found myself getting my neck in all sorts of weird positions, to see the Spanish Peaks as long as possible. Now, we have to wear seat belts and I'm an adult in the passenger seat, heading west. I wish I could have been the kid again, facing out the back window. I would have had a much better view.

LaVeta Pass was beautiful, too. Every turn was a new discovery. I'm pretty sure my jaw was stuck open, in awe of a part of God's Country I had never been to before. It was a beautiful drive to the turnoff to our cabin. It was in a gated community. The owner lives in Texas. Why would someone own a cabin in Colorado and live in Texas? My brain could not comprehend that at all! It was a winding, six-mile drive on a little dirt road to the cabin. We passed other cabins and when we drove down the rocky, bumpy road to our cabin, I was a happy kid again. This cabin was a whole single house, not a motel or look-alikes, like in Cascade. It was pretty secluded. Inside was so awesome. It was small, but big enough for us. It was super cozy and had everything we could possibly need or want--food in the cupboards, washer and dryer, bathrobes for the hot tub, wood stove, at least a zillion movies, and a great stereo. One of my favorite parts—a loft with a log bed and furniture. I always wanted a loft and log furniture in my dream cabin! My friend is afraid of heights, so she didn't fight me for the loft. She had her own little room with a log bed and furniture. The deck was pretty awesome—looking at the mountains right there around us. Again, that air! The deck had a grill, table, and OU chairs. That's the only problem I had. Being a K-State Wildcat fan, OU is an enemy! They were comfy, though. I spent a lot of time out there, writing. Nighttime was amazing, too. Total darkness, except for the clear night sky with a gazillion stars and a beautiful full moon. We found an oldies station on the radio. Played the songs we listened to in junior high and high school. We cried to some of them. We missed each other so much all those years we couldn't find each other. I knew she was dead. I couldn't find her anywhere. And how awesome is it that during those 32 years she was looking for me, too? Is that true friendship or what? We missed out on so many life events—divorces, births, deaths, graduations, marriages, grandkids. But, it was like we were never apart. Ever. Our circumstances are different. Our lives are totally different. Our kids' and grandkids' lives are totally different. But, one thing is the same. She's still the practical one (like Ron) and I'm still the crazy dreamer. Oh, yeah, she's still taller than I am and I'm still short. Mutt and Jeff. That's what my parents always called us. Those few days, just hanging out and catching up, were so precious. Just like old times when we were inseparable. Now, almost every day we send each other a message at least, if we can't talk on messenger or on the phone.

One of the days we drove to Alamosa to ride the scenic train. Well, it left the station without us and there wasn't another one that day. That was another beautiful drive. We could see the sand dunes from the road, and Mt. Blanca was beautiful. We had the same station on the radio—listening to the songs that made us cry. Doesn't take much to make me cry anyway. It was a fun drive back to the cabin, the deck, the hot tub, the beauty, the air…

The time in Colorado was not long enough. I felt peace. I felt an awesome connection to God and even asked my friend how anyone could look at the mountains and not believe in God? That reality stuff really is not nice sometimes. The day came when we had to leave. I had to catch the train from Garden City that night. She had a two-hour drive after my train left. I hated leaving the cabin. Since the road was very windy, I couldn't look back and it was out of sight quickly. I didn't want to leave. But, we had to. So, my friend drove away. I forced my neck into all different positions, trying to look at the Spanish Peaks and LaVeta, as we drove away. At least this time I was on the passenger side going east, so it was easier.

We had a lot of time to kill, so we stopped in Walsenburg to look at shops and eat lunch. The place where we ate lunch was so cute and the food was very yummy. It was very hot that day. The people in the shops didn't have air conditioning—only fans. They all said it was unusually hot there. We had fun looking around at the shops. Then came the part I really dreaded. Leaving Walsenburg meant leaving the view even more. We were sad, driving away. Driving east when our hearts were west. It was a great few days and we hated to leave there. We also knew the hard part would be leaving each other in Garden City. Me on Amtrak. Her driving to Oklahoma. I knew we had been to some special places. But, I had no clue what God was up to. He is amazing and He just blows my mind away sometimes—OK, always.

We took our time going back to Garden City. Eventually, it was time to go to the train station. I had decided I wasn't even gonna attempt to stay in my seat. I put my duffle bag and suitcase on this huge shelf-like place right inside where I got on. No way was I going to try and find my seat in the dark and attempt to put my things above the seats of people who were sleeping. I was still short and the overhead place was still over my head. So, without my luggage, I found my seat. I had two seats to myself. So, I got comfy for awhile, but couldn't sleep. Found the window car again and hung out there for the majority of the five or six hours. I found my seat again and tried to sleep, but couldn't. So many things were going through my head. Colorado, LaVeta, the cabin, the people at Lucy's, at the shops…if only they knew the impression they made on us. My friend loves Colorado. But, she doesn't feel the tug that I feel. I cannot begin to understand how someone does not feel a tug there!

So, I thought about the people in the towns we went through, the people who were sleeping on the train. Were they happy? Sad? Excited? Dreading leaving someplace, too? Or dreading going someplace? Were they married? Single? Divorced? Have kids? Grandkids? Dogs? Were they widows? Widowers? Were they going to a wedding? Funeral? What were their stories? I really wanted to know these people. But, since it was in the middle of the night again, no one wanted to talk to me. I wouldn't ever see them again. Oh, yeah, I never had cell service that whole trip! No one back here got the honor of seeing my pictures, hearing my story. The sun was starting to come up again. This time, I was going east and seeing the sunrise better. As always, God is the Creator of masterpieces when it comes to sunrises and sunsets. I smiled and told Him "thank you". I watched it go from sunrise to daytime. Ron's mom and dad were waiting for me when I got there. I was very happy to see them at 6-something AM! I was thankful they came to get me so early. I love them so much. Even though I was happy to see them and would be happy to see my animals, friends, and family again, my heart was still in LaVeta, Colorado.

# June 7, 2014

It's so weird how things happen. I have always wanted to live in Colorado. Was always afraid to move there on my own, as a single parent. There were always the "what if's" and fear to stop me. I have longed to wake up every morning to an awesome view and fresh mountain air. And then watch the sunsets and stars and thank Him for letting me be in God's Country. Because of fear of moving to a place where I didn't know anyone and having my two kids, I stayed in Kansas. After my divorce, when my daughter was two, my sister and I lived in Manitou for a summer. That was not a good part of my life. Had to move back to Kansas. Guess it just never was the right time to move there after that. I always wanted to, though. But, I had my son, went to K-State, was blessed to have worked in the field I wanted for 12 years, found Ron—all that—so was meant to be here. Since last summer, I have really missed LaVeta. Like being super homesick—even though that was the only time I've been there and it wasn't even for very long. I've felt that tug—that I belong there. The Spanish Peaks, LaVeta--that image is ingrained in my brain. I feel that God is sending me there. He's answering my childhood prayers to live in God's Country. I don't understand His timing. Why did He wait till I'm 55 years old? Is it because I needed to do the things I did all these years? Good and bad decisions. I didn't know about listening for God to tell me what to do and when. Now, I know to do it and I now am feeling total peace. I feel He is leading me to LaVeta to live. I feel He put me through losing Ron to lead me to a relationship, love, and trust with Jesus that I never had before. I am not afraid of how things will happen, or when. I now trust that God will make things happen in His time. He will work out the details. I feel He took Ron away from me, but gave me the support of many awesome people. I feel he told me to write this book, to use my pain to help others somehow. And to help me heal. I feel He put the people in my path to help me with this book. I feel that I am to stay here until I do whatever needs to be done to get this book published. Whenever that happens, it's like this chapter of my life is done. My time here in Topeka will be done. It will be time to start a new chapter of my life in LaVeta, Colorado, and to start a new book about God sending me there. So, stay tuned to see how God did all this! When I first told my friend about I Love Lucy RV Park, I told her I really felt like either there was someone there we needed to meet, or someone there who needed us. I still feel that way, only stronger. I feel it's where I belong. I tell people about it and they think I'm crazy. Either they don't believe in God, so they don't understand how I feel He is working all things out. Or they just know I'm a dreamer and figure it's another of my wild dreams that I won't make happen. No, I'm not making it happen. God is and will. Just like when I felt I was being told to go to the Holy Land and writing a book about it. That hasn't happened yet, but I think He was giving me a heads-up that I'm going, but just "not yet". And the awesome thing about moving to LaVeta is that I am not afraid now. That feels incredible. I'm not worried about any of the how's or what if's or if my car will really make it. I know God will work out the details and tell me what to do, how to do it, and when. He will be in the driver's seat. And, like one of my very favorite Bible verses, Jeremiah 29:11, says, "for I know the plans I have for you", declares the Lord, "plans to prosper you and not to harm you, plans to give you hope and a future" (NIV). That's all I need to know, right there. I will be OK. God's got my back.

# June 11, 2014

So, like the title of this book says—God Never Wastes a Hurt—it's beginning to make sense how God has used all my past hurts for His Good and His Glory. He is answering my prayer from years and years of wanting to live in God's Country.

I didn't have a clue how this book would end. People told me God would tell me when it's done, and how to end it. I didn't understand how it could end because it's about grieving, mourning, and growing in my faith. There's no ending date saying I'm done grieving or I'm all done growing in faith. That isn't possible. I really thought this book would just be the only one. Then, there will be the one about the Holy Land, whenever that happens, and I cannot wait for that time when God sends me there. My mother-in-law mentioned that maybe this should be a series. I liked that idea, but didn't know how to do it. Then, God told me this book is done. It is finished. It's time to start the next one about how He works out the details of LaVeta. How He shows me how to trust Him in all this and so my faith will grow even stronger. Maybe the trip to Colby, driving there alone, was to show me I can do it. It isn't as far as LaVeta, but over halfway. Maybe the trip to Excelsior Springs is to go to the places Ron and I did on our honeymoon and be at peace with him being gone. And to show me that even though there won't be anyone I know waiting for me there, God will be there. He will be with me all the way to LaVeta. He will be there when I get there. I have so many questions about what will happen there. Will I get to open a little shop like I have also dreamed about? Will I find some job? Will I just live off disability and be free to spend my time writing, exploring God's Country and experiencing all the beauty He created, and write about it? When will He show me why LaVeta is where I belong, out of all the places in Colorado? What about my loved ones here? Will my kids move, too? Will they understand why I gotta go? Will my car make it? Can I afford it? So many questions! But, again, this is all about trust and faith and depending on Him to let me know what to do and when. It's about me paying attention, listening, and being obedient. Just like Ron was. God knows how it's all gonna work out. He wrote the story, He knows the ending.

So, today, I will start a new book about my journey to LaVeta, Colorado. I can't wait to see how He directs me and works out the details. Moving won't happen for awhile, at least not till Spring. A lot can and will happen in that time. A lot of growing, healing, grieving, and whatever else He puts in my path.

I pray whoever has read this book has laughed, cried, had to think about something, and has either learned something about grief or about faith. And how God Never Wastes a Hurt.

# Jan. 9th, 2018

Before this book goes to print soon, I want to add that there are places in this book where I talk about God taking Ron away from me. I am sure there will be some of you who do not agree with me.

I understand that God doesn't take away from us. He does, however, allow bad things to happen. Those were my feelings at the time this book was written in 2013 and 2014. I thought about changing those words, but it did not feel like the right thing to do. This is my journey, my experience and my emotions about grief, faith and hope.

I am also sure that some people who have experienced the death of a loved one may have felt this same way in their grief journey and I do not want to take away how they may also feel.

After being in prayer and having others pray with me, I believe when bad things happen and God's people leave this earth, He takes those people to be "Home" with Him and with Jesus, who is seated on His right side.

Printed in the United States
By Bookmasters